CHAIM POTOK

A Critical Companion

Sanford Sternlicht

CRITICAL COMPANIONS TO POPULAR CONTEMPORARY WRITERS
Kathleen Gregory Klein, Series Editor

Greenwood Press
Westport, Connecticut • London

Library of Congress Cataloging-in-Publication Data

Sternlicht, Sanford V.
    Chaim Potok : a critical companion / Sanford Sternlicht.
        p.   cm.—(Critical companions to popular contemporary writers, ISSN 1082–4979)
    Includes bibliographical references (p.   ) and index.
    ISBN 0–313–31181–1 (alk. paper)
    1. Potok, Chaim—Criticism and interpretation.   2. Judaism and literature—United
States—History—20th century.   3. Jewish fiction—History and criticism.   4. Jews in
literature.   I. Title.   II. Series.
PS3566.O69Z88   2000
813'.54—dc21   00–035343

British Library Cataloguing in Publication Data is available.

Library of Congress Catalog Card Number: 00–035343
ISBN: 0–313–31181–1
ISSN: 1082–4979

First published in 2000

Greenwood Press, 88 Post Road West, Westport, CT 06881
An imprint of Greenwood Publishing Group, Inc.
www.greenwood.com

Printed in the United States of America

The paper used in this book complies with the
Permanent Paper Standard issued by the National
Information Standards Organization (Z39.48–1984).

10 9 8 7 6 5 4 3 2 1

Contents

Contents

Series Foreword

The authors who appear in the series Critical Companions to Popular Contemporary Writers are all best-selling writers. They do not simply have one successful novel, but a string of them. Fans, critics, and specialist readers eagerly anticipate their next book. For some, high cash advances and breakthrough sales figures are automatic; movie deals often follow. Some writers become household names, recognized by almost everyone.

But, their novels are read one by one. Each reader chooses to start and, more importantly, to finish a book because of what she or he finds there. The real test of a novel is in the satisfaction its readers experience. This series acknowledges the extraordinary involvement of readers and writers in creating a best-seller.

The authors included in this series were chosen by an Advisory Board composed of high school English teachers and high school and public librarians. They ranked a list of best-selling writers according to their popularity among different groups of readers. For the first series, writers in the top-ranked group who had received no book-length, academic, literary analysis (or none in at least the past ten years) were chosen. Because of this selection method, Critical Companions to Popular Contemporary Writers meets a need that is being addressed nowhere else. The success of these volumes as reported by reviewers, librarians, and teachers led to an expansion of the series mandate to include some writers with wide critical attention—Toni Morrison, John Irving, and Maya Angelou, for example—to extend the usefulness of the series.

The volumes in the series are written by scholars with particular expertise in analyzing popular fiction. These specialists add an academic focus to the popular success that these writers already enjoy.

The series is designed to appeal to a wide range of readers. The general reading public will find explanations for the appeal of these well-known writers. Fans will find biographical and fictional questions answered. Students will find literary analysis, discussions of fictional genres, carefully organized introductions to new ways of reading the novels, and bibliographies for additional research. Whether browsing through the book for pleasure or using it for an assignment, readers will find that the most recent novels of the authors are included.

Each volume begins with a biographical chapter drawing on published information, autobiographies or memoirs, prior interviews, and, in some cases, interviews given especially for this series. A chapter on literary history and genres describes how the author's work fits into a larger literary context. The following chapters analyze the writer's most important, most popular, and most recent novels in detail. Each chapter focuses on one or more novels. This approach, suggested by the Advisory Board as the most useful to student research, allows for an in-depth analysis of the writer's fiction. Close and careful readings with numerous examples show readers exactly how the novels work. These chapters are organized around three central elements: plot development (how the story line moves forward), character development (what the reader knows of the important figures), and theme (the significant ideas of the novel). Chapters may also include sections on generic conventions (how the novel is similar or different from others in its same category of science fiction, fantasy, thriller, etc.), narrative point of view (who tells the story and how), symbols and literary language, and historical or social context. Each chapter ends with an "alternative reading" of the novel. The volume concludes with a primary and secondary bibliography, including reviews.

The alternative readings are a unique feature of this series. By demonstrating a particular way of reading each novel, they provide a clear example of how a specific perspective can reveal important aspects of the book. In the alternative reading sections, one contemporary literary theory—way of reading, such as feminist criticism, Marxism, new historicism, deconstruction, or Jungian psychological critique—is defined in brief, easily comprehensible language. That definition is then applied to the novel to highlight specific features that might go unnoticed or be understood differently in a more general reading. Each volume defines two or three specific theories, making them part of the reader's understanding of how diverse meanings may be constructed from a single novel.

Taken collectively, the volumes in the Critical Companions to Popular Contemporary Writers series provide a wide-ranging investigation of the complexities of current best-selling fiction. By treating these novels seriously as both literary works and publishing successes, the series demonstrates the potential of popular literature in contemporary culture.

Kathleen Gregory Klein
Southern Connecticut State University

Acknowledgments

This book has evolved from my work in the Judaic Studies program of Syracuse University. I wish to thank a colleague of mine in the program and in the English department, Harvey Teres, for recommending me to Greenwood Press as a possible author of a work on Chaim Potok. Another colleague, Ken Frieden, who holds the B. G. Rudolph Chair in Judaic Studies at Syracuse University, has helped me with information and translations from Hebrew and Yiddish.

I owe much to my two undergraduate research assistants, Susan Hodara and Lane Roberts. My partner Mary Beth Hinton, a fine editor, has helped me with my rewrites, and I thank her for that and for her support during the months of evenings I sequestered myself behind a pile of books and articles and a clicking word processor. Librarian Wendy Bousfield has helped by obtaining books for me, and the Interlibrary Loan Department of Bird Library, Syracuse University, as always, facilitated my research.

Of course, I thank Rabbi Chaim Potok for his kindness in supplying his photograph, for offering his assistance, but most of all for writing a body of work that has given me much knowledge, understanding, and pleasure.

The Life of Chaim Potok

Chaim Potok is a modern Jewish American writer who has no quarrel with his religion, but who has continually explored the conflict between Jewish values and culture and the values and culture of the secular American world within which the Jewish sphere exists. As a rabbi who writes fiction and nonfiction, he understands and illustrates that "American Judaism comprises forty-five percent of world Jewry, [but] it is by no means a monolithic, religiously informed group. It is, rather, composed of many strands—religious and ethnic—all of which are attempting to cope with modernity" (Berger, 37). As a philosophical writer he is concerned with the question of the suffering not only of the Jewish people but of any individual persons who are innocent and good. He addresses, by implication, the age-old question of theodicy: How can God's justice be validated in the face of the evil the Deity permits to exist?

CHILDHOOD

Chaim Potok's father, Benjamin Max Potok, came to America from Poland after serving in World War I with a contingent of Poles in the Austrian army fighting the Russians. At the end of the war he returned home to a strange reward, a savage attack on a Jewish community: a

Polish pogrom. He decided to come to "the Golden Land," America, where he worked as a jeweler and watchmaker in the then mostly Jewish section of the Bronx borough of New York City. He married Mollie Friedman, who was also a Jewish immigrant from Poland. The couple devoutly followed the faith of their ancestors as ultra-Orthodox Jews. Benjamin, although he did not wear the prescribed garb, considered himself a Hassid, a member of the most traditional part of the Jewish religious community.

Their son Herman Harold Potok was born 17 February 1929 in the Bronx and, as is the custom for many Jews, was given a Hebrew name too. His is Chaim Tvzi. He grew up an observant Orthodox Jew like his parents and became a rabbi, a philosopher, and a significant American writer. As a grown man, Potok noted that he had spent his childhood deeply immersed inside a Jewish world, "with a child's increasing awareness of his own culture's richness and shortcomings" (Potok, "Culture Confrontation in Urban America," 161).

As a child Chaim Potok received a parochial primary education in Jewish schools in the Bronx called yeshivas. Besides required secular subjects, the curriculum centered on the beginning study of the Talmud, the sixty-three books of Jewish religious and ethical law based on the Hebrew Bible, and the teachings of great rabbis.

Like millions of other people in America, Chaim's parents struggled through the Great Depression (1929–1939). The Potoks' section of the Bronx was then populated primarily, but not exclusively, by working-class Jews, many of whom lost their jobs in those hard times. Small-business people like the Potoks also suffered and struggled to get by. African Americans and Italian, Polish, and Irish immigrants and their children shared both the neighborhood and the hard times. Potok "saw poverty and despair, and I remember to this day the ashen pallor on my father's face that night in the late Thirties when he told us we would have to go on welfare" (Potok, "Culture Confrontation," 161).

Potok's near ghettolike childhood environment was often dangerous, especially for a studious Jewish boy: "The streets were on occasion dark with gang violence and with the hate that had made the sea journey from the anti-Semitic underbelly of Europe" (Potok, "Culture Confrontation," 161).

The gravest terror for young Chaim Potok, and indeed for his family, came from World War II and the slow, terrible, unfolding realization that under Hitler—the most virulent anti-Semite in the history of the world—Germany was systematically destroying European Jewry. The thought that the mass murder of people, only because they were Jew-ish—a program called genocide—brought terror to the dreams of Jewish children in America. If the Allied armies could not stop the Germans, then the children and their parents would also go to the gas chambers and the crematoriums of death camps. Potok could not, would not, forget the Holocaust. That event, the greatest crime of the twentieth century, informs or is background to almost all of Potok's writing.

Chaim showed an early talent for drawing and painting, but in the Orthodox community the practice of art was considered a waste of time and perhaps even sinful. He found another channel for his creativity: writing. His parents and relatives could better understand the urge to write, for, after all, their faith was founded on the Hebrew Bible—the written word of God—and the entire community was literate even if their reading was mainly limited to the sacred texts of their religion.

EARLY READING

Fortunately for the world of literature Chaim, at the age of fourteen, came across English writer Evelyn Waugh's great novel, *Brideshead Revisited* (1945). This story about the life of a religious, aristocratic English Catholic family seen through the eyes of an outsider who wanted to be a part of that secure and appealing life—his best friend's life—influenced Potok's view of himself as an outsider to American life: one wanting to participate in that culture while remaining true to the traditions and values of his own heritage. Similarly, Potok's early heroes would look with fascination and sometimes envy across the culture chasm that sep-arates from secular American life the extreme practitioners of Jewish Orthodoxy—the Hasidim, with their black hats and coats, full beards, and sidelocks of braided hair.

Potok attended the Talmudic Academy High School of Yeshiva Uni-versity in Washington Heights, Manhattan, for his secondary education, which was Orthodox, not Hasidic, and therefore less extreme. Mean-while, he had fallen in love with the power of the creative imagination as it uses the written word to re-create the past, preserve the present, seemingly give birth to new lives, and phrase the moral dilemmas per-ennially facing humankind.

After reading *Brideshead Revisited*, Potok embraced a regimen of read-ing serious secular modern novelists like James Joyce, Ernest Heming-way, William Faulkner, and the German genius Thomas Mann. These masters of the modern novel significantly influenced the budding author. Potok acknowledged his debt to Joyce's great novel about the boyhood and maturation of a writer, *A Portrait of the Artist as a Young Man* (1914). Potok was attracted to the book when still in his teens because Joyce deals with "an individual at the heart of his Catholicism encountering elements from the very heart of Western civilization" (Kauvar, 292). He stated that Joyce "was very close to what I'm trying to do" (Kauvar, 292). So Potok began to consider the possibility of a career as a writer of fiction in which he could tell the story of, and interpret to the general American public, the culture of his parents and his own generation of more secular American Jews.

COLLEGE, THE RABBINATE, AND MILITARY SERVICE

Potok enrolled in Yeshiva University in 1946, a school with a rigorous program combining the liberal arts and sciences with intensive theological study. He began to write articles and short stories for the university yearbook and eventually became its editor. He received a bachelor of arts in English degree in 1950, graduating summa cum laude. At Yeshiva the strands of secular education and a love of literature, as well as further religious studies, entwined and have ever since structured Potok's intellectual and creative life. At Yeshiva he made the critical decision to move his affiliation in the spectrum of American Jewish religious practice from Orthodox fundamentalism to the more centrist, more worldly Conservative Judaism.

After Yeshiva Potok entered the Jewish Theological Seminary of America in New York City to study for the Conservative Jewish rabbinate. Once again he was an outstanding student; his many prizes included the Hebrew Literature Prize and the Bible Prize. In 1954 he was awarded the master of Hebrew literature degree and was ordained as a Conservative rabbi. Potok had moved from the extreme right to the center of American Judaism. This move caused relatives and some friends from the Bronx to ostracize him as an apostate, a betrayer of his faith. Potok had to rebuild his life.

Although as a clergyman Potok did not have to serve in the military during the Korean War, he was and is a patriotic American, and so he volunteered for army service as a combat chaplain in Korea. He worked with a forward area medical battalion, (like a M*A*S*H unit without the comedy), attached to a combat engineer battalion. Potok served in Korea from the winding down of the conflict in 1955 to 1957. Attending to soldiers of all faiths, Potok was deeply moved by the shared humanity and the similar values and needs of all young soldiers. This experience would provide background and experience for Potok's fifth novel, *The Book of Lights* (1981), in which two young friends begin their lives as rabbis by serving in Korea as chaplains. While still in Korea, Potok began four years of work on an army novel about the beleaguered Asian country, following the path of best-selling Hemingway-like World War II writers such as Norman Mailer, James Jones, and Irwin Shaw. But his war novel never found a publisher. In 1992 *I Am the Clay* would come out of Potok's post–Korean War experience.

EARLY EMPLOYMENT, GRADUATE SCHOOL, AND MARRIAGE

Instead of seeking a congregation when he left the army, Potok decided on a career in education. He accepted a position as a Jewish studies instructor at the University of Judaism in Los Angeles and taught there from 1957 to 1959. Simultaneously, he directed a California year-round Conservative Jewish camp, Camp Ramah. In 1958 Potok married Adena Sarah Mosevitzky, a psychiatric social worker. The young couple moved to Philadelphia in 1959 so that Potok could begin graduate work in philosophy at the University of Pennsylvania. He was also appointed scholar-in-residence at Philadelphia's Har Zion Temple. That four-year salaried appointment helped Chaim and Adena financially as they were expecting their first child, their daughter Rena, born in 1962.

FIRST WRITINGS

Despite an enormously crowded schedule, Potok finished his novel of Korea, put it aside, and started on his second. After seven years and several drafts this work became *The Chosen* (1967). This story of the conflict between Hasidic and Orthodox Judaism in the 1940s, played out in the relationship between a Hasidic youth and an Orthodox boy, begins in rivalry and ends in deep friendship and mutual understanding. This book, Potok's first published novel, became a best-seller, was nominated for a National Book Award, and established the author as a significant American writer as well as interpreter of American Jewish culture. *New*

Republic reviewer Philip Toynbee noted that "[f]ew Jewish writers have emerged from so deep in the heart of orthodoxy; fewer still have been able to write about their emergence with such an unforced sympathy for both sides and every participant" (21).

The popularity of *The Chosen* was due in part to something that was happening in America, indeed in the Western World. The Cold War had come upon us, troubling the Western democracies; one result was a revival of religion and religion-based writing. Charles I. Glicksberg in *Western Humanities Review* ascribed the reason specifically to "the unsettled condition of the world, the unsettling threat of another world war, the bankruptcy of the Marxist . . . vision, the revolutionary changes that have taken place in the scientific outlook, the splitting of the atom and the manufacture and use of the atomic bomb" (75). Many people, especially the young, took to new means of dealing with despair such as involvement in the drug culture, an embrace of oriental religions or existentialism, and, for some, a return to traditional Western religions and their values.

ISRAEL

In 1963 Potok took his family to Israel for a year. Part of the motivation for the sojourn was to make time to finish his doctoral dissertation, "The Rationalism and Skepticism of Solomon Maimon." Maimon was an eighteenth-century Jewish scholar who lived in Poland but went to Germany to study the great philosophy of the time and to publish his own concepts and interpretations. In moving to Israel Potok also wanted to distance himself from and gain perspective on the urban Jewish community he was writing about in *The Chosen*.

But mainly, Israel beckoned Potok because he desired, as did most intellectual American Jews of his generation, some firsthand experience with Zionism. That nationalist movement began in 1897. As widely recognized by historians, with the establishment of the State of Israel in 1948, Zionism became the great historical and emotional experience of World Jewry in the twentieth century, second only in significance and meaning to the Holocaust. For most religious Jews, Zionism represents not only the reconstitution of a Jewish national state for the first time since the second century A.D., but also a fulfillment of the biblical prophecy of the return to the Promised Land, bitterly and sadly longed for over nearly two millennia. Many Jews today believe that this return to the homeland by the Jews precedes the coming of the Messiah, a God-anointed holy person who will relieve the Jewish people of their historic suffering and rebuild for them in their own land the great Temple of Jerusalem destroyed by the Roman army in 70 A.D. Christians, of course, believe that Jesus Christ is that Messiah.

BROOKLYN

Refreshed and profoundly moved by his creative sabbatical in Israel, Potok brought his family in 1964 to the heart of the Hasidic world, Brooklyn. To earn his living and support his family he accepted a faculty appointment at the prestigious Teachers Institute of the Jewish Theological Seminary of America where he had studied for his master's degree ten years before.

In Brooklyn Potok was close to the most extremely religious Jewish community in the world, the Hasidim. Hasidism was brought to America just before and shortly after World War II, first by Jews fleeing growing persecution in Poland and then by concentration camp survivors and other Holocaust victims. These refugees had once been a part of a very large community in Poland and Ukraine who, in their worship of God, kept themselves separate from all other Jews.

The Hasids still do maintain that separation that is a key to their survival and their continuity. They experience Judaism with joy and emotion, with ecstatic singing and dancing, instead of with strict and rabbinical Talmudic learning. The tradition was begun in the eighteenth century by the followers of the Baal Shem Tov, a saintly man whose name is translated as "The Master of the Good Name."

Potok, as a Conservative Jewish rabbi, was considerably removed from the Hasidim, who are philosophically and politically to the right of the Orthodox. But Potok was and is fascinated by their fervor, exclusivity, and singular values. He has great respect for Hasidic life, and he admires their ability to survive, even to thrive, in environments that range from difficult to threatening. His desire to understand and to love the Hasids is a major motivation for Potok the novelist and the person.

EDITOR

In 1965 Adena and Chaim's second daughter, Naama, was born, and Potok was awarded the doctor of philosophy degree from the University of Pennsylvania upon the acceptance of his dissertation. He then went to work with the Jewish Publication Society of America, while making his final revisions of *The Chosen*, published in 1967. Potok had been made editor in chief of the publication society in 1966, and he remained in that capacity until 1974 when he became a special projects editor.

The Chosen received some negative comments in the Jewish press but was welcomed with great appreciation by the general reading public, most Jewish readers, and the national press. It received the Edward Lewis Wallant Prize for Jewish fiction and spent thirty-nine weeks on the *New York Times* best-seller list. Four hundred thousand clothbound copies of *The Chosen* were sold and more than three million paperbacks.

In 1968 the Potoks had their third and last child, their son Akiva. Potok had already begun writing his second published novel, *The Promise* (1969), a sequel to *The Chosen*. It continues the story in the earlier novel of the young men in conflict as they move into their respective careers and struggle to keep family antipathies from destroying their friendship. Richard Freedman in the *Washington Post Book World* said that *The Promise* has "a glow of human erudition and compassion" (3). This novel received the Athenaeum Award.

When his next novel, *My Name Is Asher Lev*, came out in 1972, Potok was contemplating another, longer sojourn in Israel. The new novel tells the story of an artist seeking an identity in a society from which he is beginning to isolate himself. The move to Israel with his family for a period of four years came out of Potok's own painful struggle as an artist and a philosopher to find a world in which he could truly fit. For the moment, it did not seem to exist in America, where he was living on the razor's edge between a Jewish community he respected but which did not value his work and a Jewish community that valorized his novels but seemed shallow and lacking in commitment to its historical inheritance. In reviewing *My Name Is Asher Lev* the *New York Times* critic Guy Davenport stated, "Potok has a sure sense of how to diagram tragic misunderstanding. He knows that it must happen in a context of faith and love, and that it must be the exercise of faith and love that breaks hearts" (5).

TO THE HOLY LAND AGAIN AND RETURN

In 1973 the Potok family once again settled in Israel, living in Jerusalem, the capital of the country and the sacred city of the Jews, a city three thousand years old. The Potoks lived there for four years and then returned to the United States to reside in Philadelphia, where Potok once more took employment with the Jewish Publication Society of America—this time as special projects editor. To this day Potok makes his home primarily in a large house in a pleasant Philadelphia suburb. Yet he maintains an apartment in Jerusalem, where he returns for refuge from the more material American culture and for the spiritual revitalization that only prayer at the Western Wall of the ancient Temple can bring to a Jewish person with a profound belief in God. His novel *In the Beginning* appeared in 1975 while the Potoks were still living year-round in the Holy City of the Jews.

Set in the second quarter of the twentieth century, this novel is the story of a bright Jewish boy who, like Potok, is brought up in the Bronx and becomes a scholar of the Hebrew Bible. He has poor health and is overly protected by his religious parents and bullied outside of the home by other, bigger boys. The Great Depression of the 1930s nearly ruins his family. The hero, David Lurie, is accident prone, and he feels that he is a jinx to his family because of their seemingly bad luck, as when David's mother trips on the way home from the hospital with him. David is tortured by bad dreams brought about by the rise of Hitler and German anti-Semitism in the 1930s and the destruction in Europe brought about by World War II. The world seems meaningless and this is devastating to a person brought up in a devout household; the main question of *In the Beginning* is how is one able to maintain faith in the seemingly Godless world of the early twentieth century. H. J. Keimig, writing in *Best Seller*, calls the book "a classic story of a Jewish family and their friends told by a master of narrative fiction" (302).

In 1978 Potok published his first nonfiction book, *Wanderings: Chaim Potok's History of the Jews*, in which he makes "an effort to see how I related to the cultural package called Judaism, and its beginnings" (Pfeiffer, 55). His approach was to provide a Jewish history that communicates, as a rabbi might, by being both scholarly and popular. The coffee-table book with many beautiful illustrations nevertheless tells a painful story of a numerically insignificant people bound to the Bible who have had to spend almost all of their history enduring persecution by succeeding civilizations that, miraculously, they have survived.

Of course, Potok was reflecting on his own and his family's wanderings from Europe to America, from America to Korea to America again, from America to Israel and back again, from the Bronx to Brooklyn to California to Philadelphia. On a spiritual level, Potok journeyed from the Hasidic Judaism of his father to Orthodox Judaism to Conservative Judaism. From the reflective immersion in history that came with the research on *Wanderings*, Potok surfaced as a different novelist.

THE MORAL NOVELIST

The redirected writer embraced more openly and fully what he saw as moral, ethical, and spiritual questions. Additionally, and in relation to these thematic queries, Potok specifically chose in *The Book of Lights*, published in 1981, to explore Jewish mysticism. He desired to comprehend a world in which good and evil coexist and even comingle, as when science devises an atomic bomb to end a terrible war and kills tens of thousands of people at Hiroshima to achieve that end.

The dark, ambitious novel is the story of a young religious Jewish man, Gershon Loran, whose parents were killed in Jerusalem and who now lives with relatives in a poor section of New York City, where he sees a vision one night on a rooftop. He decides to study mysticism through the Kabbalah, a system of interpretation of the Hebrew Bible devised over several hundred years in the Dark and Middle Ages that assumes every letter in the Bible has an occult meaning. The study of the Kabbalah is counterpoised to the study of the Talmud, the record of the Oral Law of the Jews based on ancient rabbinical commentary. In other words, the study of the Kabbalah was devised to spiritualize Judaism.

THE VISUAL ARTIST

Potok never abandoned his early love and need for painting, for visual art, which was and is for him yet another way to reach the spiritual in himself and sometimes even to see into the souls of others. He paints as an expressionist: intuitive, spiritual, and expressive of deeply felt emotion. His subjects range from introspective self-portraits to landscapes, still lifes, and nudes. He has had successful exhibitions since 1979. Potok also is adept at photography, but considers it merely a hobby. His photographs sometimes serve as the base study for painting to come later.

THE MOVIE

Motion pictures greatly increased America's awareness of Chaim Potok. In 1982 the movie version of *The Chosen* was released. The distinguished film actor Rod Steiger played Reb Sanders, the major father figure in the novel. The director was Jeremy Cagen, and Potok was chosen to write the screenplay. The success of the film increased critical interest in Potok's fiction and brought him many new readers. Audiences were deeply moved by the film, and they found the novel equally satisfying; they were intrigued by the detailed, colorful, sociological depiction of Jewish life in America.

COLLEGE TEACHING

Potok has always valued and loved teaching: he has a calling for higher education. In 1983 Potok joined the philosophy department of the University of Pennsylvania as a visiting professor teaching the philosophy of literature, thus able to instruct in the two academic subjects nearest his heart. He also was a visiting lecturer at nearby Bryn Mawr College in 1985 and at Johns Hopkins University in 1994, 1996, and 1997.

THE LATER NOVELS

Potok's sixth novel, *Davita's Harp*, was published in 1985. It marked a distinct departure from the point of view of the author's earlier work; this time the narrator is a female, Ilana Davita, who relates the story of her life from age eight to fourteen in the 1930s and 1940s. She is a child of a mixed marriage. Her parents are committed communists, and they are disappointed because Davita is determined to think and decide for herself, looking for truth and the meaning of life in both the Jewish and Christian traditions. *Davita's Harp* is also different from Potok's five earlier novels because Judaism is not a central theme in the story. Marcia R. Hoffman in *Library Journal* found that Potok had "insight into the mind and heart of an adolescent girl" and that he provided a "splendid evocation of the period" (180).

The Gift of Asher Lev appeared in 1990, winning the National Jewish Book Award. A sequel to *My Name Is Asher Lev*, the novel is concerned with the perennial conflict between the artist and conventional society antagonistic to his or her product and way of life. Asher Lev has been exiled from his Hasidic community for twenty years, living in France with his wife and children. He returns to his old Brooklyn community to deal with the death of a beloved uncle and to seek reconciliation with the religious community of his youth. Brian Morton in *The (London) Times*

Literary Supplement noted that "The novel . . . heralds a new sophistication in Potok's art, which in the past was short on humour and reticent about whole areas of experience, notably the erotic" (1182).

Potok's eighth novel, *I Am the Clay*, followed in 1992. The author abandons as his setting the Brooklyn Jewish community of the 1930s and 1940s for the country of Korea, where he did his military service in the 1950s. The story takes place as the Korean War is winding down. The hero, Kim Sin Gyu, is an orphan whose parents and extended family have been killed in the conflict and whose village has been destroyed. The tale is an archetypal one of the innocent refugee struggling to survive in a world devoid of humane values and seeming to have gone mad with a lust for destruction. Jackie Gropman, in *School Library Journal*, called *I Am the Clay* "a simple and powerful narrative of survival of the human spirit" (148).

In 1996 Potok directed his cultural and historical knowledge and narrative skills to the writing of the history of a Jewish family surviving Imperial Russian and, later, Soviet persecution when he published *The Gates of November: Chronicles of the Slepak Family*. Potok, as a friend of the family, acquired access to the family records and used them as raw material for a nonfiction narrative beset with a father-son conflict. Critical reception to this history was positive. *The Gates of November*, as with all Potok books, has been translated into many foreign languages.

CHILDREN'S BOOKS

Potok has been a teacher all of his adult life—after all, the English translation of the word "rabbi" is teacher. So it is not surprising that Potok the storyteller, now a grandfather, has written two books for children and one for adolescents. Working with Tony Auth, Potok published *The Tree of Here* (1993) and *The Sky of Now* (1995). The first of these two books for children is about a family that is moving. A boy named Jason is happy with his friends and school, but his father has been promoted and now the family must pack up and move—a common dilemma for American children. Jason is disappointed, frightened, and upset; but under the shelter of a large dogwood tree in the yard, he is able to express his anxiety. The tree is a good listener, and Jason feels better. Jason is part of a strong family, and *The Tree of Here* is filled with family warmth.

The Sky of Now is about Brian, a boy afraid of heights who learns to face his fear. A trip to the top of the Statue of Liberty is ruined because he fears falling. How can he overcome the fear of height when he wants to fly airplanes? Fortunately, his uncle helps him to conquer his fear. The moral of the book is that irrational fear can be overcome at any age. Potok has also published a collection of short stories for teens: *Zebra and Other Stories* (1998).

PLAYWRIGHTING

Although a musical version of *The Chosen* had opened in New York City in 1988, it was not until the decade of the 1990s that Potok became interested in the dramatic form. He has written *Out of the Depths* (1990), *Sins of the Father* (1990), and *The Play of Lights* (1992). In March 1999 a dramatic version of *The Chosen*, written by Potok with the collaboration of Aaron Posner, opened in Philadelphia. Potok's plays have not proved commercially successful so far, but they are of interest to his fans, as are his short stories.

At the age of seventy Potok, an active person in good health, remains fully engaged in literary pursuits. He is a bearded, intense man, five-foot-eight, with deep-probing brown eyes. He dresses like a professional: a philosopher, a spiritual leader, a professor, and, most of all, a distinguished writer. Readers around the world await additional powerful narratives and explorations of moral and ethical dilemmas from this American master who remains committed to his belief in the Almighty as he explores the commanding relationship between the Deity and the Jewish people.

2

Chaim Potok's Literary Heritage and Achievements

Chaim Potok chooses to write stories about the American Jewish community, the religious traditions of the Jewish people, the discomfit conservative religious people of all faiths feel toward the aesthetics of Western culture, the materialism and lack of idealism in capitalist societies, the suffering caused by historical and contemporary anti-Semitism, and the need for spirituality in Western civilization. The fact that he is so learned in Jewish history and so informed by contemporary Jewish American life has given him a unique place in modern American writing. Potok is a conservative in lifestyle, religion, and writing, and his foregrounding of Aristotelian values such as emphasizing plot and character have made him one of the most accessible novelists of the last half of the twentieth century.

WHAT IS A JEWISH AMERICAN WRITER?

Some History

Jews first came to the Western Hemisphere with Columbus and other early Spanish explorers. The Dutch colony of New Amsterdam, later New York, received Jews in the 1640s, and these people became successful merchants and good citizens under Dutch and then British rule.

After the American Revolution, Jewish communities thrived in the cities of the Eastern seaboard. These Jewish people worshiped in the Sephardic tradition; that is, praying in the forms of Judaism that came out of ancient Spain and the Muslim world. Besides English, they spoke an ancient form of Spanish called Ladino. These early American Jews were very few in number, and many of them eventually assimilated into Christian America.

In the mid-nineteenth century large numbers of Jews joined other immigrants fleeing revolution and repression in the middle European countries and settled in Eastern U.S. cities, where in a generation many also realized the American dream and became successful in business and the professions. They spoke German as well as English. They, and all subsequent Jewish immigrant groups, worshiped in the Ashkenazic tradition of medieval Europe, with ceremonies somewhat different from the earlier Sephardic immigrants.

Towards the end of the nineteenth century, a mass migration of mainly impoverished Jews from Russia and Poland began. Although some left because of the economic opportunities available in the United States and Great Britain, the exodus was largely fueled by anti-Semitism and massacres of Jewish men, women, and children in those countries. As many as two million Jews emigrated to the United States, settling in ghettolike areas of large Eastern cities, areas that had housed earlier immigrant groups like the Irish and the Germans before them. These Jewish immigrants spoke Yiddish, a language closely related to German. They not only had to learn English but also had to adapt to a very different culture. The largest number came to New York City between 1882 and 1924. They took up residence on the Lower East Side of Manhattan until prosperity and a lessening of anti-Semitism gave many of them the opportunity to join mainstream America and move into suburban communities. It is from this immigrant population that almost all Jewish American writers descended.

First Generation

The most important of the early Jewish American writers came from Czarist Russia or Austrian Poland in the late nineteenth century or very early in the twentieth century. The first were Abraham Cahan (1860–1951) and Anzia Yezierska (1880?–1970). The former came from Vilna, Lithuania, to New York. He was a socialist thinker who learned English after Yiddish and Russian and who became the senior editor of the most important Jewish language newspaper in America, *The Daily Forward*. Cahan wrote the first important Jewish American novel, *The Rise of David Levinsky* (1917). This book established the main theme for much of Jewish American fiction to come: the conflict between the values of Judaism brought over from the old country with the raw materialism and Darwinian survival of the fittest struggle of American life.

Yezierska came from Russia and learned English on the Lower East Side where she worked at menial jobs. Despite terrible poverty she took advantage of educational opportunities and became skilled in writing English. Her talent was a natural one, and she published several popular novels and short story collections. Her work, especially *Hungry Hearts* (1920) and *The Bread Givers* (1925), became well known because she was the first Jewish American writer whose stories were filmed in the Hollywood of the silent film era.

Yezierska's main theme was the exploitation of immigrant women by American society, including Jewish American society. Her secondary theme was the advantage taken, even abuse, of immigrant Jewish wives and Jewish children by religious Jewish men, who used their patriarchal power and their desire to study as an excuse to avoid earning a living for their families. Instead they forced their wives and children to toil to support them.

Second Generation

The next generation of Jewish American writers, children of immigrants, is best exemplified by Michael Gold (1893–1967) and Henry Roth (1906–1995). Gold, a dedicated communist, wrote what is considered to be the most inflammatory Jewish American novel ever published, *Jews without Money* (1930). It is the story of the suffering of an impoverished immigrant family living on the Lower East Side of Manhattan at the beginning of the twentieth century. Living conditions are crowded beyond belief. People are hungry. Landlords, bosses, and politicians exploit the immigrants. They get sick, they have accidents, they die violent deaths. The novel ends with an impassioned call to the masses to change the society that has so cruelly exploited all workers and their families.

Roth, in his first novel, *Call It Sleep* (1934), wrote the acknowledged masterpiece of Jewish American immigrant literature. It is a stream-of-consciousness narrative in which the text consists of the thoughts and experiences of the narrator. It owes much to the literary techniques of James Joyce and Virginia Woolf. This generation of Jewish American writers was very aware of the literary traditions and styles of the great contemporary writers writing in English on both sides of the Atlantic Ocean.

Call It Sleep is narrated by an immigrant child whose father hates and torments him because he is suspicious that the boy is not really his son. The boy's mother strives to protect him from the persecution of his father but she too is a victim of his mad jealousy. Mother love, such a strong, binding emotion in Jewish life and art, sustains the youth. The novel marks the advent of Freudian psychology into the Jewish American novel.

The World War II Generation

The leaders of the next generation of major Jewish American writers proved to be the most influential on American fiction writing in general: Bernard Malamud (1914–1986), Saul Bellow (1915–), Herman Wouk (1915–), and Philip Roth (1933–). Malamud's novels, like *The Assistant* (1957) and *A New Life* (1961), explore Jewish identity and ethics through characters struggling and mostly failing to get beyond their fear of Gentiles and their misgivings about cross-culturalization.

Bellow, who won the Nobel Prize for Literature in 1976, has written novels like *The Adventures of Augie March* (1953), *Herzog* (1964), and *Mr. Sammler's Planet* (1970) in which Jewish men, young and old, struggle, usually unsuccessfully, to survive the destructive elements in American life.

Wouk, a World War II warrior writer, initially wrote against military despotism but depicted Jewish activism as well in *The Caine Mutiny* (1951). He went on to write *Marjorie Morningstar* (1955), the sociological depiction of a Jewish American girl who is made vulnerable by the weakening of her Jewish identity. More recently Wouk has written a massive, Tolstoyan two-part narrative of World War II, *The Winds of War* (1971) and *War and Remembrance* (1978). These novels deal with the causes of the war and the crimes committed by the Axis nations—Germany, Italy, and Japan. They were primarily but not exclusively written from a Jewish perspective, for the main theme in the novels is the terrible suffering of the Jewish people at the hands of the Germans and their collaborators.

Roth has been the most provocative of all Jewish American fiction writers because he has chosen to depict the unpleasantness of assimilation and to satirize and even chastise his middle-class coreligionists for their selfish materialism, hypocrisy, ludicrous airs, and sexual lust in such novels as *Portnoy's Complaint* (1969) and *The Professor of Desire* (1977). Because Roth began to publish major fiction as early as 1959, he is the transitional figure between the World War II Jewish American writers and those who came later.

Potok's Generation

The contemporary Jewish American writer who comes closest to Potok in the intensity of Jewish identification and concern for moral and ethical considerations is Cynthia Ozick (1928–   ), whose novels like *The Cannibal Galaxy* (1983) and *The Messiah of Stockholm* (1987), draw on Judaism for moral energy and authority, and whose characters seek ways to keep their religion and still be part of the surrounding world.

A Jewish American writer may be defined as an American writer with a Jewish background—immigrant or native born—who identifies as a Jew and incorporates aspects of the life of Jews in America into his or her work. Their stories are informed at least in part by Jewish history, memory, culture, ethics, and values.

Potok is a Jewish American writer because he is committed to traditional Judaism in an American version. His settings are primarily within Jewish communities. His profound themes center on the problems of being ethical Jews within the Christian world. And his major characters live lives shaped by the tragedies and glories of Jewish history.

THE JEWISH COMMUNITY IN AMERICA

The readers of Chaim Potok's novels need to be informed about the divisions in contemporary Judaism because these divisions are a part of the tensions and familial conflicts that constitute a major subject in the novels.

Hasidism

A minor but very visible division of the approximately five million American Jews, Hasidic Jews live worshipful lives congregating about specific, revered rabbinical leaders. These leaders derive their authority from Eastern European sects founded in eighteenth-century Poland and Ukraine during a mystical revival when many Jews felt that the religion had become too dry, sterile, and academic. Hasidic Judaism is extremely right wing. Its proponents regularly proselytize among other Jews, whom they consider to have deviated from true Judaism, while avoiding association with the majority American Jewish population and all other Americans. Hasids dress in garments fashioned after those worn by Eastern European Jews in the eighteenth century and consequently are sometimes mistaken for Amish people and vice versa.

Modern Orthodox

A large majority of world Jewry, a population of fourteen million, consider themselves orthodox although not all carry out all the tenets of their affiliation. Orthodox Jews consider themselves the mainstream of the religion. They worship God and live within the Talmudic tradition of the great rabbis, which began before the destruction of the Temple of Jerusalem by the Romans in 70 A.D., and the dispersion of the Jewish people throughout the world. It continues in the far corners of the world. Orthodox Jews unself-consciously consider themselves the perpetuators of the unchanged ancient religion of the Israelites. They keep the Sabbath and the Ten Commandments. They eat only Kosher food. Women generally worship apart from men.

Conservative

The Conservative movement in American Jewry is a liberal version of Orthodoxy, one that embraces more contemporary intellectualism. Like all other divisions of American Judaism it spans a spectrum of ritual requirements, but Conservatism allows Jews to be more comfortable in general with mainstream American life. It is more active in the social sphere than Orthodoxy. There is some question today as to whether Conservative Judaism or Orthodox Judaism represents the majority of American Jews actually practicing their religion.

Reform

Reform Judaism evolved before Conservatism. It came to America from Germany early in the nineteenth century. It is highly intellectual and active in community affairs. Its practices, such as men and women praying together, often seem more closely related to left-wing Protestant denominations like Unitarian/Universalists than to the more traditional divisions of Judaism. Reform numbers are small but the congregations, often consisting primarily of professionals, academics, artists, and other community leaders, are quite influential and community minded.

Reconstructionists are believers who do not accept that the holy texts are God-given. They emphasize the historical culture and continuity of Judaism.

Secularists

It may be that in reality a majority of the five million American Jews, among whom are many who call themselves Conservative or Reform Jews, are in fact nonattendees at synagogues and temples who do not keep the rituals of any group whether it is to honor the Sabbath in a traditional way, study holy books, keep a kosher kitchen, eat only allowed and kosher (ritual regulated and certified) food, and in one form or another pray to God regularly. Indeed many Americans, proud of their Jewish identity, their ancient history, the contributions of the Jewish people to world culture, science, philosophy, and religion, and the accomplishments of the State of Israel, consider themselves Jews and stand with their religious brethren even if they are agnostics. They join with the large number of Americans who are unaffiliated with a religious organization and call themselves secular humanists.

LITERARY INFLUENCES ON POTOK

The Holy and Spiritual Books

As a writing rabbi, Potok naturally is much indebted to, and eager to employ, the holy books of Judaism, the most significant source of inspiration and the main study of his lifetime. The spiritual quests of his heroes and heroines are within the context of their religion. The holy books of Judaism are a part of the structure of Potok's novels in that they stand like marble columns, firming content and meaning with their not-to-be-questioned moral authority.

A most significant achievement of Potok is his brilliant incorporation, in narrative and symbol, of biblical themes, Jewish ethical disputations, and the distilled essence of the profound texts of the "People of the Book." Potok states that he is "committed to the notion that theology and behavior must be organically related. A theology that is not linked directly to a pattern of behavior . . . is a macabre game without words. And a pattern of behavior that is not linked to a system of thought is an instance of religious robotry" ("The State of Jewish Belief," 172). Thus, in becoming a widely read and popular writer, Potok made the great books of Judaism relevant to contemporary American readers.

The Hebrew Bible

The Hebrew Bible, the writing of which commenced in the tenth century B.C. under King Solomon, is the greatest achievement of the Jewish people, a foundation stone of Western civilization, and the most important gift to the Christian and Muslim worlds. It forms the basis for the moral and ethical strictures of those religions and is a part of their progressive historical development as well as their cosmological view of God's relationship with humankind.

The Hebrew Bible differs slightly from Eastern Orthodox, Protestant, and Roman Catholic versions in the number and order of books. It is divided into three parts: Torah, translated as Teaching or Law; Neviim, translated as Prophets; and Ketuvim, translated as Writings. The latter section is the least important. Neviim (Prophets) complements Torah, but it is Torah, the first five books of the Bible, that by far is the most important part of the Bible for Jews.

The Torah

The five books—Genesis, Exodus, Leviticus, Numbers, Deuteronomy— that open the Torah contain the profound story of the Creation, the early Israelites' acceptance of monotheism, and the great escape, under the leadership of Moses, from the tyranny of Pharonic Egypt. The basic Jewish code of civil and religious law is contained in the Torah.

The Talmud consists of sixty-three books that contain further religious, civil, and ethical ramifications of Jewish law. The Talmud is based on oral interpretations of the Bible and on the teachings of very early rabbis. When finally written down about 200 B.C. the collection was named the Mishnah. As other great rabbis studied and wrote commentary on the Mishnah, their words and judgments were also recorded. This collection is called the Gemara. Therefore the Talmud is composed of the Mishnah and the Gemara. In fact there are two Talmuds, one called the Babylonian Talmud and one the Palestinian or Jerusalem Talmud. The former, composed around 500 B.C. in the period of the Babylonian captivity of the Israelites, has garnered the greater respect and authority.

The Babylonian Talmud with the Hebrew Bible itself are the backbone of Jewish religious practice and philosophical thought. For twenty-five hundred years these two texts have sustained and regulated practically every aspect of Jewish life.

The Kabbalah

"Kabbalah" is translated as tradition. The word is a general term for Jewish mysticism that came into being in the Middle Ages. Originally part of the oral tradition of Jewish study and now available in various textual permutations, it remains of great interest to students of the spiritual and occult. The Kabbalah claims secret knowledge including an oral version of the Torah given to Moses by God and passed on to some people in succeeding generations as a way to communicate mysteriously but directly with God, bypassing the Talmud and other rabbinical manifestations of Jewish law. Scholars who begin a study of the several medieval texts become fascinated with the imagination and ingenuity in the writings of the mystical sages.

THE MODERN NOVEL

Chaim Potok was born into the cultural milieu called Modernism, an epoch that came about in revolt against the Victorian values and restrictions of the nineteenth century. The modern novel in America is best exemplified by the works of Ernest Hemingway, F. Scott Fitzgerald, and William Faulkner. These early modernists remained basically true to the long tradition of realism and careful storytelling. Other modern novelists chose experimental styles like expressionism (depicting subjectivity and emotions) or stream-of-consciousness writing in their attempt to disassociate with everything that seemed old-fashioned and bourgeois. They also tended toward elitism, as if the only readers worth cultivating were highly educated people at ease with the experimental.

Potok learned his craft by studying modern literature in college and reading the novels of modernist writers both in and outside of school. He read the realists and the experimentalists, but in the end he chose the more conservative approach. Nevertheless he has maintained his modernist credentials with his sparse style, his unobtrusive authorial voice, and his sensitive use of contemporary psychological theories.

Uniquely, Potok continually reminds us that the novel has always had social and moral dimensions. Whereas other modernists have devoted themselves to the assault on taboos in published writing such as the depiction of explicit sex or the embracing of politically extreme, radical ideologies, or the endorsing of materialist values, Potok's modernist innovation is, interestingly, retrograde, reintroducing the centrality of religious faith in the lives of vast numbers of people living within the cultures of the industrialized world. Religious faith in Potok does not, however, relieve the believer from the complexities of modern life. It is a part of it.

As in James Joyce's *A Portrait of the Artist as a Young Man*, a novel Potok has said was instrumental in his development as a writer, Potok's heroes are moving, sometimes slowly, from one world to another—that is, from a religious community to a secular one. The experience is painful but full of learning opportunities. Joyce's youthful, autobiographical hero, Stephen Dedalus, struggles with his family, church, and society and finally breaks away from insular Ireland to pursue the life of a poet in the wider world of the European continent.

The journey to intellectual freedom often comes at the cost of strained father and son relationships, but fathers often inadvertently or consciously have prepared their sons or daughters to live with what Potok calls "core-to-core" confrontations. He brings together characters who see the world from within and through their own cultures. He has them confront each other in the wider, secular, world inhabited by both groups. The confrontation is enlightening for characters and readers alike because it often leads to understanding and sometimes even to tolerance.

CULTURE CLASH IN THE LAND OF OPPORTUNITY

Chaim Potok is the son of Jewish immigrants. In the late nineteenth century and throughout the twentieth century Jews came to America for two reasons: to escape religious persecution and to participate in the American Dream. People all over the world then and now are aware of the great economic opportunities that America has made possible, and they are aware that American society has provided for more upward mobility than most. The dream has been expressed simplistically in the Horatio Alger tales of a poor young man making good and the rags to riches legends that advertise American capitalism.

But in truth there are no ghetto walls here, and competence, skill, integrity, and hard work erode or break down other social, cultural, and racial impediments sooner or later. Still, strongly religious communities like Orthodox American Jewry and especially the Hasidic community, struggle to prevent the materialism and secularism of the Land of Opportunity from diverting the young from the required allegiances and devotions. Worst of all for orthodox and fundamental communities is the fear that the young will leave the community altogether, through the embracing of ideas and values found in secular education or through intermarriage.

Defensively, fundamentalists discourage contact with people outside the religious community. If the larger society will not wall them in, they build the wall themselves to keep the larger society out. They load the available time of the young with additional studies and rituals, and they go to great lengths to maintain strict gender separation so that sexual interest is repressed. This culture clash made possible by the availability of choice is the central conflict in the novels of Chaim Potok. Potok says: "Culture interaction is my subject." He works "from the cores of cultures in confrontation" ("The First Eighteen Years," 103). What Potok believes and has shown in his novels is that it is possible to have both an enriched secular life and a Jewish life in America. The message is optimistic, especially for a people who have not had that opportunity through most of their history.

WRITING STYLE

In speaking of a writer's style, one is considering the way the writer uses language to paint the scenes of the narrative, to weave the plot, and to bring characters seemingly to life. Style is a very individual thing. Some writers are particularly admired as "stylists." Their craft is so finely tuned that their writing is foregrounded when critics evaluate them. Some writers may even eschew meaning and significance in their search for beauty of expression.

Chaim Potok is not that kind of writer. Of course he uses imagery, both figurative (comparison expressions like metaphors) and literal (direct descriptions). He can paint a desert picture as when he explains: "The high god of the Bedouin was the moon, by whose silver-white light he grazed his flocks and whose benevolence cooled the air and moistened the ground. Once I saw a full moon rise over Arabia on a chill April night: no, it seemed to leap from its underground cavern . . . and I could sense how it might be worshipped as a god, this life-giving lamp that replaced the killing sun of the day (*Wanderings*, 249).

Symbols

Potok's diction, or use of words, is neither formal nor colloquial but a direct and comfortable blend of both possibilities. At his sharpest, Potok sounds like this:

> "How the world drinks our blood," Reb Saunders said. "How the world makes us suffer. It is the will of God. We must accept the will of God." He was silent for a long moment. Then he raised his eyes and said softly, "Master of the Universe, how do you permit such things to happen?"
> The question hung in the air like a sigh of pain. (*The Chosen*, 191)

Note also the rhythm of the prose, how it flows easily from the page to the eye, and how it serves both to reveal a character's feeling and with a single sentence—"Then he raised his eyes and said softly"—paint his sorrowful face.

Of course Potok uses symbols—signs made of words that carry deeper meaning beyond the literal, as in *The Chosen* when a softball, an American symbol if there ever was one, hits a young Jewish boy close to the eye, and the meeting between the struck pitcher and the batter develops into a lifelong comradeship. An eye-opening moment in the youth's life (36). But Potok's use of rhetorical devices is deceptive. Beneath the simplicity and the straightforwardness lies deep thought and great understanding of human nature.

Potok's writing style can be summarized as direct, spare, and very carefully produced. He has said to Edward A. Abramson: "Each of the novels was rewritten four or five times from start to finish; sections of them were rewritten more than a dozen times. I work very hard to achieve that simplicity of style. There is a great deal concealed beneath that simplicity" (141).

The depth and profundity of Potok's study of the Bible, the Talmud, and many other Jewish texts have influenced his creativity and writing style to the extent that he as a Talmudist weighs all sides of the issues he confronts with his narratives. He understands the complexity of human issues and human beings. And he rounds out his characters with a polishing that comes from great compassion for individual human beings. In Potok's own words, he writes "from *within* Judaism" ("The State of Jewish Belief," 171).

ACHIEVEMENT

The publication of *The Chosen* in 1968 "startled the literary world . . . with the knowledge that something new had entered American writing" (Harap, 163). A Jewish American novelist in the post-immigration period had chosen with great success to write about the fundamentalist part of American Jewish society instead of the usual population of Jewish American novels: assimilated, secular humanist Jews. Yet despite the fact that Potok had moved away, in a political sense, from Hasidic values, he never denigrates Jewish fundamentalism or fundamentalists.

Furthermore, Potok took a traditional theme in American literature, the father-son conflict—such as the one in the grand drama by his fellow Jewish writer, Arthur Miller, *Death of a Salesman* (1949)—and entered it in the Jewish American novel. Potok knew Miller's play, and he also realized that although Miller does not specify, the garment center salesperson Willy Loman and his family are Jewish. Taking a cue from the dramatist, Potok relieved the depiction of the Jewish family of the burden of improbable saintliness. Like Miller's, Potok's families have internal dissents and moral and ethical crises.

Chaim Potok is an affirmative writer. He is not sardonic. Irony and satire are not his forte. He believes that there is goodness in almost all people and that life is precious, good, and very worth living. In presenting the cultural confrontation between traditional Jewish values and American material life, he offers the conclusion that American life is enriched by Jewishness. In return, Potok implies, American freedom, equality, and opportunity have given the Jew in America the unique historical chance to challenge the strictures of the past and to find individual paths to spirituality under a God who seems more understanding and forgiving than the Deity constructed by closed-minded theologians in the past.

3

The Chosen
(1967)

The title, *The Chosen*, refers to the belief of the Jewish people that they are God's chosen people, chosen to bring to the world monotheism, as well as God's words, messages, and will through the Bible. They also believe that they were chosen to be "a light unto the nations"; that is, a standard setter for ethical and moral behavior and for the promulgation of justice and mercy.

Surely for many Jewish people and perhaps for Potok the appellation "The Chosen People" is tinged with irony, considering the long history of the persecution of Jews throughout much of the world. Indeed the chronological period of the novel is the time of the Holocaust, the greatest disaster in Jewish history except perhaps for the destruction of the Temple and the city of Jerusalem in 70 A.D. But the time of the novel also encompasses the return of the Jews after almost two thousand years to Israel, the land that God promised Moses would be their eternal homeland.

The narrator of the book is the teenager Reuven Malter. The focus is an enemy youth, Danny Saunders, who becomes his friend. The subject of the book is the developing friendship between two young men from opposing communities and the way their friendship overcomes the impediments placed in their path by their contemporaries and by members of the older generation.

A tightly controlled, carefully crafted novel, *The Chosen* is set in Williamsburg, a section of Brooklyn where two Jewish groups, Hasids and Orthodox worshipers, live in proximity but with little to do with each other because of religious differences. The time of the novel runs from early 1944 through World War II and ends in 1948 with the founding of the State of Israel. Two boys begin a long and fruitful relationship with a violent act. Danny Saunders, the son of a Hasidic leader and a star hitter on his Hasidic parochial school softball team, aims a vicious line drive at the pitcher, Reuven Malter, the son of an Orthodox schoolteacher and scholar, and a star player for his Orthodox parochial school. The ball hits Reuven on the face just above his eye. His eyeglasses are shattered and a piece of glass enters his eye.

The remorseful Danny visits Reuven in the hospital and the latter is forgiving. The enemies become fast friends even though they are from different worlds. Although Reuven narrates this first-person novel, it is mostly about the inner torment and conflict the brilliant Danny suffers as he comes to realize that he does not wish to succeed his father as the rabbinical leader of their Hasidic sect. His intelligence is propelling him into the secular world where he will study Freud and become a psychologist.

Reuven is the catalyst that helps his friend, Danny, to become his own person. The community conflict between the two groups of Jews is set against the background of the vast conflict of World War II in which, ironically, while these Brooklyn Jews are in conflict, the Germans are destroying European Jewry.

The scenes of *The Chosen* include Brooklyn tenement homes, synagogues, schools and school yards, and a New York City hospital in the 1940s.

PLOT DEVELOPMENT

The Chosen is divided into three books. The first has four chapters; the second has eight chapters; the third contains six. The total number of chapters is eighteen. The number eighteen is written in Hebrew with the character for the letter Ch'ai. The word for the number is the same word as the word for "life." The letter/number is often worn around the neck as a good luck talisman. The Hebrew/Jewish toast is "l'chayam." It means "to life." That there are eighteen chapters in the book is not a coincidence when the author is a student of Jewish holy and mystical books, especially the Kabbalah, and whose Hebrew name is Chaim. The novel is a paean to life and it ends with optimism. Jewish life goes on in America, and the younger generation is solid and well prepared for success and leadership. Neither the books nor the chapters are titled.

The Chosen opens in a very dramatic way. It is June 1944. The world is at war. In Brooklyn a softball game between two parochial school teams of Jewish boys turns into a holy war, and if the reader thought that the American Jewish community is homogeneous he or she quickly learns differently. The narrator, fifteen-year-old Reuven, attends an Orthodox parochial school. He and his schoolmates do not desire to set themselves apart from the wider American community. Rather, they intend to go to college and either become rabbis or professional people like doctors, lawyers, or business people.

The opposing team is from an ultra-Orthodox Hasidic parochial school. The boys wear clothing and hair styles that set them apart. For the most part they plan to go into small businesses where they can control their time so that work does not interfere with their religious obligations. Unfortunately, the Hasidic youth disparage the other Jewish boys as what they call *Apikoros*, a word translated as apostates although it originally came from the word "Epicurean," or people who enjoyed worldly things over spiritual ones.

The two groups of boys are at extreme variance over religious, political, and social matters. Later in the story the two groups nearly will come to blows over the issue of whether Jews should support the new state of Israel or wait for the coming of the Messiah who will lead them home again. Youths like Reuven and their parents can't wait. That the boys are playing a softball game, a quintessential American sport, signifies that the conflict is actually over before it began. American ways, perhaps one could say the values and ways of Western culture, will win out for people like Reuven, who represents the vast majority of American Jews. After all, even the Hasidic boys want to be "baseball heroes" in each other's eyes and in the eyes of their rivals.

As the game progresses in the school yard, the players become more and more aggressive. The softball game becomes a miniwar. The ultra-Orthodox Hasidic boys led by Danny believe they are the righteous ones and their merely Orthodox opponents, led by Reuven, are lost sinners. Reuven's coach, Mr. Galanter, directs his team as if the game were a battle in the war going on at the time: World War II. Reuven pitches to Danny who purposely hits a vicious line drive at Reuven's head. The

ball strikes Reuven's upraised glove and is deflected, but the upper rim
of his eyeglasses is hit and a piece of glass is driven into his left eye. The
pain is very great and Reuven is rushed off to the hospital in a taxi.

One of the suspenseful plot lines of the novel is built on the possibility
that Reuven may lose the sight in one eye. A skillful ophthalmologist,
Dr. Syndman, removes the piece of glass in a delicate operation and,
more than 100 pages later, pronounces the eye healed as the scar tissue
has not covered the pupil.

In the hospital Reuven seethes with hatred for Danny Saunders. Having been informed of the injury to his son, Reuven's father, David Malter,
rushes to his bedside. He is a secondary-school teacher in an Orthodox
yeshiva, a publishing scholar on the Talmud and general Jewish studies.
Reuven's mother is dead.

The next day, on a second visit, Mr. Malter informs Reuven that
Danny's father Reb (Rabbi) Saunders, has been calling to express his
concern and sympathy for Reuven and to inform the Malters that Danny
is very sorry for what has happened. Reuven is doubtful of Danny's
sincerity.

While Reuven is in his hospital bed, his eye heavily bandaged, D-Day
arrives. The Americans, British, and Canadians land on the Normandy
coast of German-occupied France. As great historical events are taking
place the injured Reuven is contemplating his future. His father wants
him to be a mathematician as he is very good in math, but Reuven thinks
he prefers to be a rabbi.

Suddenly Danny appears at Reuven's bedside. The injured youth is
amazed. Danny believes that Reuven hates him, and Reuven lies and
says he doesn't. But he can't restrain himself, and he curses Danny, hop-
ing to inflict guilt on him. Sorrowfully, Danny leaves, and it is Reuven
who begins to feel a little guilt. He has even frightened himself with his
anger and hatred. Regret seeps in and Reuven is unable to sleep.

The next day Danny comes back and Reuven is more civil. He is curious about his ultra-religious opposite, and he apologizes for his rudeness and anger. To Danny's surprise the lonely patient is happy to see
a youth his own age. Quickly they use each other's first names and a
friendship, something both boys need, begins. They are both wounded
but in different ways: Reuven by the injury and the fear of loss of sight
in one eye and Danny, as it turns out, by the coldness of his father.

Reuven is surprised that Danny speaks English perfectly. He thought
the Hasids only knew Yiddish well. The youths begin to compare their
education and Reuven learns how hard Danny, a prodigy of learning

with a photographic memory, must study to satisfy his father, a Hasidic sect leader. When Danny sees Mr. Malter in the hospital he is greatly surprised because he never realized that the kind, intellectual man who has been helping him by directing his reading choices in the public library is Reuven's father. Mr. Malter, wise as well as generous, had never let on to the bright boy in Hasidic garb that he knew his identity.

Reuven's father wants him to make Danny his friend. Unlike Reb Saunders Mr. Malter is committed to bringing the different and differing Jewish communities together in the face of the common enemy: world fascism. Malter understands and takes pain to inform his son of Danny's background. He informs his son that the Hasidic community's isolation from influences that might negate its coherence and its all-consuming obsession with worshiping God helped it survive in an Eastern Europe historically full of murderous hatred for the Hasidim.

Simultaneously, as Malter informs his son of European Judaism's tragic history, Potok informs his readership. We later learned that Reb Saunders saved his community by leading them out of Russia after World War I and bringing them to America so that they missed being victims of Hitler's Holocaust.

Malter explains further that Reb Saunders is a great scholar of the Talmud and that he is reputed to be a man of compassion, and that Danny Saunders is a phenomenon, with so brilliant a mind that he is able to read quickly down the center of a page of complicated text and understand everything on that page. Yet he seems to have no one to talk to of his own age. Compassionately, Mr. Malter wants Reuven to be the friend that Danny needs so badly, and it is Reuven, a fine scholar himself, who will also benefit by a relationship that comes to seem preordained.

As Reuven begins to attend Hasidic services with Danny and to eat with Danny's family, he learns to respect Reb Saunders and even like the family, especially Danny's fourteen-year-old sister. Quickly though, Reuven is apprised by Danny that the girl is already contracted to marry a young Hasidic man selected by their parents. Reuven then no longer thinks about her. Danny's mother is also a background character, essentially providing food for her family. The descriptions of the feasting of the Hasidim point out the importance of food in that culture.

What Reuven, and one presumes Potok, finds less appealing are the unkempt houses, the neglect of decoration and little amenities like flowerpots, and the rudeness of Hasidic people on the street as when burly men bump into others in desperate attempts to avoid accidental contact with contaminating women. Reuven will never be able to feel anything but an outsider in the Hasidic community even though he comes to understand it well and respect it. To him it is a twilight world, something primitive, almost savage, and the atmosphere and behavior, especially in the synagogue, seems carnivalesque.

Danny is continually queried and challenged by his father, who seems more intent on building up his son's reasoning and debating ability than on creating a loving relationship with him. Reuven comes almost to enjoy watching the father and son's intellectual battles, and Reb Saunders is happy that Reuven is Danny's friend, for the Rabbi will use Reuven to learn what secular—and therefore contraband—books Danny is reading. Reuven is an honest person, and he cannot and will not lie to the father of his friend. Reb Saunders is hurt that his son is coming under the influence of Freud and Darwin, but he takes it as God's will. Through Reuven he will try to communicate to his son what he is unable to say directly.

Background to the maturation of the two young men and the growth of their friendship is the continuation of World War II, especially in Europe. Oddly, in neither religious community do the young men ever think about the possibility that they might be called to fight in a year or two, and no other member of either community seems willing even to contemplate risking life or limb in defense of their liberty. The coach of Reuven's team, Mr. Galanter, speaks in military metaphors, preparing his players for "battle" with the Hasidic team, but later when asked why he is not in the army, in embarrassment he states that his desire is to serve but that he is not healthy enough to do so.

By the time of the Battle of the Bulge in December 1944 the high-school students are seeing little of each other, enmeshed as they are in their serious studies and preparation for college. The war in Europe comes to an end, and news of the Holocaust comes through to shock the minds and the hearts of the people of the free world. A flu epidemic has stricken Danny Reuven, and Mr. Malter has been hurled into a deep depression by the revelation of the horror of the German death camps.

Within days of learning of the extent of the Holocaust, Mr. Malter suffers a heart attack and is hospitalized. Reuven cannot be alone except for a housekeeper coming in to make meals, and so Reb Saunders invites him to live with his family and share a room with Danny until his father recovers. Reuven is generously accepted as a member of the family, and the two friends are united for a few summer months.

Whenever Reuven visits his father in the hospital, the main topic of discussion is the destruction of European Jewry and the indifference of

Western democracies, like Britain and the United States, to their fate. It is as if the Holocaust continued to claim victims like Mr. Malter who are both horrified and depressed by the unfolding reality of genocide on an unprecedented scale. They suffer in sympathy and sorrow.

In the autumn of 1945 Mr. Malter has recovered. The war has ended with the dropping of atomic bombs on Hiroshima and Nagasaki. The young men, as they had planned, enroll in the same school, Hirsch College, a combination seminary and secular institution in Brooklyn. Danny studies psychology as well as Talmud. He is able to read Freud in the original German. More and more he feels desperately trapped by his father's dream that he will succeed him as leader of the sect.

Danny excels in Talmudic studies at the college but is frustrated with a psychology department that is only interested in experimental psychology as a function of physiology and does not recognize the importance and value of Freudian psychoanalysis. A small rift develops between the friends because Reuven, with his strong background in mathematics, agrees with Danny's teachers that Freudian theory is based on unscientific, inductive logic. The methodology if not the theory is flawed.

A great conflict tears Hirsch College apart. Teachers and students who are ultra-Orthodox believe that only the Messiah can reestablish the ancient State of Israel. They oppose Zionism, the nationalist movement to establish a Jewish homeland in Palestine. The Zionist students and faculty support the establishment of the new state. Many questions arise and are debated: Can an American Jew have allegiance to the United States and to Israel simultaneously? What would a Jewish person do if America and Israel went to war with each other?

Like his father, Reuven is a Zionist. Danny does not join either side although his heart is with the Zionists. But Danny is not allowed to continue communication with his friend. Reb Saunders has forbidden it. The Malters' Zionism was the last straw. The friendship was cut off. But the always wise and compassionate Mr. Malter understands and explains to his son that the fanaticism of people like Reb Saunders has kept Judaism alive through two thousand years of persecution.

For months the two college students are in constant proximity but never speak to each other. Reuven feels only hatred for Reb Saunders, who has deprived him and Danny of their close companionship. In 1947 the United Nations voted for partition of Palestine into two states, one Jewish and one Arab. Reuven and his father are ecstatic. Mr. Malter has worked himself to exhaustion in the cause of Zionism, arguing, making speeches, and raising funds. In Hirsch College, Zionist and anti-Zionist students are close to blows. Mr. Malter suffers his second heart attack and is rushed to the hospital. (He is frequently seriously ill but survives through both *The Chosen* and *The Promise*.) At school Danny brushes Reuven's hand with his as a gesture of understanding and sympathy, and thus the suffering of Mr. Malter restores the friendship. Even though they cannot speak to each other the young men communicate with their eyes.

In May of 1948 after a final enabling vote by the United Nations, Israel proclaims its independence and begins a life-and-death struggle with the armies of all of its Arab neighbors. With that desperate struggle going on, the anti-Zionist sentiment in the college disappears.

In September Mr. Malter is well enough to return to his teaching and his scholarship. Anti-Zionism also dies out in the ultra-Orthodox community, and in the spring of 1949 Danny is allowed to talk again to his friend. They had endured a painful silence for two years. With help from Reuven, Danny becomes more successful with mathematics and deductive, scientific logic to the point that he becomes interested in experimental psychology.

In June of 1946 Reuven is invited to the wedding of Danny's sister. Interestingly, we never learn her name. She is a daughter and a sister and then a wife, defined always by her position or relationship but never as an individual person. Reuven notes that Reb Saunders has aged considerably. The reader assumes that his defeat in the battle for the soul of the Jewish people has had a bad effect on his spirit and his health.

In their last year at college the young men affirm their commitments to their respective professions: the rabbinate for Reuven and clinical psychology for Danny after a Ph.D. Danny's younger brother is now destined to become the "tzaddik," the leader of his father's sect.

The last element in the plot's suspense is the waiting for Danny to tell his father that he is going to graduate school for psychology. In the end Reb Saunders accepts Danny's decision to go to Columbia University, and he gives his son his blessings. Danny's younger brother will be the dynastic inheritor of the leadership of the congregation. When we last see Danny he has shaved off his beard and cut his sidelocks. Other questions arise in the reader's mind. Will he remain an ultra-Orthodox Jew or does the cutting of hair symbolize cutting of roots so that Danny will join the Malters in Orthodox Judaism? Also, does the American Dream apply to those who choose to remain culturally different even if they don't dress differently? Potok's answer at the time of the writing of *The Chosen* was yes.

Reuven is deeply distressed by Danny's problems of family and conscience. He wants to help Danny, and he has learned a lesson his father has taught him, that it is not easy to be a true friend. But in the climactic scene of the novel Reb Saunders recognizes and accepts that Danny will be different from him, and he explains to Reuven that he wanted Danny to have a compassionate soul unlike the Rabbi's brother, who had a great secular mind but died in the gas chambers. The Rabbi's brother, like Solomon Maimon, the subject of Potok's doctoral dissertation, gave himself to the larger culture, the one that destroyed him. A tzaddik must stay with his people and suffer for them. For that he needs a great soul more than he needs worldly knowledge.

Danny has developed a compassionate soul because he has suffered from his need to make decisions, from the impediments placed before him, and from his father's distant coldness. It has been his good fortune to have had a friend to stand by him. Now the Rabbi knows that even though Danny will be a psychologist, he will still be a tzaddik in and to the wider world, a concerned human being with a soul. Like his father he will care for people and they will come to him also with problems. But it will be different. It will not be as a rabbi, a spiritual leader, but as a psychologist. He will not administer to their suffering souls but to their suffering minds.

The Rabbi begs forgiveness from Reuven for hating his father's Zionism, and from Danny for not being a kinder, gentler, more communicating father. The scene ends in tears of love and understanding in the eyes of the young men, and the departure of a weary old man, loved and respected too.

Danny and Reuven both graduate summa cum laude, eager and hungry for their futures. One cannot but think that although Potok denied it, he had a sequel in mind for the story of two friends full of promise and with so much of their lives yet to live.

HISTORICAL BACKGROUND

The time of *The Chosen*, as stated above, is the period between the last days of World War II and the establishment of the State of Israel. The central historical event in the novel is the Holocaust. The Holocaust, like international anti-Semitism, is considered as God's will by Reb Saunders. He sees only the truth he wishes to see: the world always slaughters Jews. For Mr. Malter and Reuven, Reb Saunders's answer is unsatisfactory and his genuine tears of sorrow are of no use. They believe the Jews must make their own answer from now on. The answer for David Malter and his son is the sovereign State of Israel, the land of refuge for the survivors of the German slaughter and for future generations who may find persecution in the countries they live in.

Reuven comes to believe with his father that Jewish survival depends on establishing a state that can defend its people. He makes the mistake of broaching the idea to the Saunders family and the Rabbi is infuriated. For Reb Saunders all other Jews are really goyim (Gentiles). Zionists would only contaminate the Holy Land. It is for the Messiah to reestablish the nation of Israel.

Mr. Malter becomes a dedicated Zionist fighting for the establishment of a Jewish state despite the opposition of the British authorities in the Palestine Mandate and the Arab population. His lesson for Reuven is that a person must make his life a meaningful one. The meaning of one's life is ultimately more important than the life itself. For Mr. Malter, there is new and more significant meaning in his life in his call to Zionism. The Holocaust can only have meaning in the concept of a universe created and watched over by God if it brings about the return of the Jewish people to their ancient land. Reuven's answer is that he will find meaning in the life of a rabbi, reorienting and reeducating secularized American Jewry. His country and his calling is America.

Potok has used history as a structural device to support his plot. The reader, although knowledgeable about the outcome of World War II and the postwar struggle of the Holocaust survivors to establish the State of Israel, nevertheless shares the suspense seemingly felt by the fictional characters living in the momentous years from 1944 through 1948. In this respect Potok's narrative relates to the work of more overt writers of historical fiction like Herman Wouk and Leon Uris.

CHARACTER DEVELOPMENT

Four characters dominate *The Chosen*: Danny Saunders, Reuven Malter, his father, and Danny's father, Rabbi Saunders. The four are skillfully manipulated by Potok as if he were composing an opera. He presents duets: Danny and Reuven; Reuven and his father; and trios: Danny, Reuven, and Mr. Malter; Danny, Reuven, and Rabbi Saunders. There is never a quartet. The fathers respect each other from a distance, and for a while Reb Saunders hates Mr. Malter for his Zionist activism, but Potok keeps them separate because their respective political positions are completely irreconcilable and bringing them together would have been so explosive as to shift the focus of the novel from the younger generation to the older.

Danny Saunders is the central character and the focus of the novel. He is a child prodigy, a genius whose father sees himself reincarnated in the brilliant son he expects will inherit the leadership of the Hasidic sect they belong to. The Hasidic congregation deifies him almost as much as his father. He is a crown prince. It is Danny who experiences the greatest change and suffers the most. He leads a schizophrenic life, secretly assimilating Western knowledge while seeming to conform to his father's image of a Hasidic leader in training (Stern, 102). It is Danny who has the greatest need for friendship and parental love. It is Danny who must confront and win out over an authoritarian if well-meaning father. It is Danny who is trapped in a free country and who must break with a smothering, stultifying tradition to learn to serve humankind in a way not approved by the fundamentalist religious sect he was born into. Psychology may become almost a secular religion for him, but he seems to have learned and accepted the limits of Freudian analysis at Hirsch College.

Restricting reading and study to Jewish law is too narrow for Danny's voracious mind. Even before the opening episode of the story he has been reading forbidden books like Charles Darwin's *On the Origin of Species by Natural Selection* and *The Descent of Man* and T. H. Huxley's *Evidence as to Man's Place in Nature*. Freud will become a passion and an obsession with him, for one of the things Danny needs to come to understand is why his father almost never talks to him except when they are studying the Talmud together. Ironically, Danny must become a rabbi even though he does not want to, and Reuven wants to become a rabbi even though he does not have to. Reuven's academic strength is in mathematics and logic, and he has already studied Bertrand Russell and Alfred North Whitehead's great book on mathematical logic, *Principia Mathematica*.

Middle-aged, thin, pale, tired, and unwell, David Malter is an idealized teacher of Jewish studies, dedicated to his Talmudic scholarship yet a humanitarian. He encourages rational explanations in textual studies. He "fuses the best in Judaic scholarship with the best in secular culture"

(Walden, 234). Unlike Rabbi Saunders and the Hasids, he believes that God is approachable to individual people. Mr. Malter knows that Western secular culture is not an enemy to Jewish life. Rather, it has much good to offer if employed judiciously. He advocates intellectual inquiry. He leads the young men to rational thinking even when the subject is religion. Jewish texts are to be explicated rationally. Jewish law must be interpreted in such a way as to blend tradition with modern ideas, scientific matter, and human needs. He is in every way an educated, tolerant, compassionate person of his time. Moreover he deeply loves his son, who is clearly the most important person in his life. Good single parent as he is, he never tries to relive his life, reach goals, or clone himself through his bright son. Mr. Malter is Potok's projection of what a Jewish parent should be.

Mr. Malter learns a very powerful, if painful, lesson in his middle age, one that Potok wishes to impress on his readership: no minority is impervious to the machinations of the larger, outside world. No people, no matter how much they love and worship God, no matter how moral and ethical their daily lives, can be passive in the matter of their own survival. Only at their peril do they live with heads in the sand—or in the sky, for that matter.

Although essentially a contemplative person, Mr. Malter is stirred to action by the awful knowledge of the Holocaust—that one third of the Jews of the world have been murdered—and he throws himself into a passionate cause for the first time in his life, the realization of Zionism in the establishment of the Jewish State of Israel. For this, like the soldier he never had to be, he nearly gives his life.

Rabbi Saunders is perhaps the most interesting and complex of the main characters in *The Chosen*. He is the charismatic hereditary leader of a religious sect that sees him as infallible and comes close to worshiping him. He is self-righteous. He eschews all seemingly frivolous discourse. He is unfeeling and cold towards his son, mistaking militant training in memorization and recall for ethical and moral instruction. He pontificates, rages, and domineers. Yet he is impotent outside his tiny principality, and all he can do for the hundreds of thousands of Hasids murdered by Hitler is weep for them and pray that the Messiah comes soon. He cannot even keep his son from being influenced by the outside world.

But in the end we have sympathy and even admiration for Reb Saunders. He does what he thinks best for his son and his dependent community. It is no easy task to serve a community that expects its saintly leader to be all-knowing and all-wise. Saunders shows compassion for Reuven when the young man is injured and when his father is ill. He suffers for what the world did to the Jewish people, and that suffering is not made easier because he believes it was God's will. Almost blasphemously, he cannot help but ask the Master of the Universe how He could permit the Holocaust to happen? And thus we can even admire and envy the surety of his pietism, seeking understanding but never doubting.

Through their characterizations Mr. Malter and Reb Saunders symbolize the struggle within the Jewish community for "possession" of the Holocaust. For Saunders and his followers it was a terrible punishment for collective sins and a test by God of the faith of His chosen people. For Malter the Holocaust was a horrible historical fact that indicated to Jews that they must take charge of their future by establishing a strong Zionist state. For him that is God's will and the destiny of the Jewish people.

Reuven is the point-of-view character representing the young Potok, observing and narrating the milieu of his childhood. He must find his Jewish identity for himself, because his wise and sensitive father is not didactic. Potok exposes his narrator to the Hasidic world precisely so that the youth can sample it, reject it as impractical and confining, and yet understand and appreciate it. We like him more than Danny. He is more human. Geniuses are hard for us to be around. Reuven will make an ideal American, not only an ideal American Jew. He will serve his community. He is devoted to his father. Unlike Danny, Reuven will follow his father's path. As a rabbi he will bring assimilated Jews back to the synagogue. He will educate their children in Jewish laws and Jewish customs. He will help to create a vitalized American Jewish community that in a sense will replace what was lost in Europe.

Reuven is a loyal friend. He is a good listener, and his counsel is generally wise and understanding. He has learned tolerance from his father, who has also taught him that a friendship should not founder on a difference of opinion. His faith in God seems unshakable, but he will not expect God to look after him. To be a good person one must do good deeds, not merely be devout. Reuven's great efforts as a student indicate determination, perseverance, and success. He is logical and scientific. Through his hospital experience and the suffering and fear his wounded eye gave him, he has developed compassion for others. Suffering has matured him as much as anything else in his life, for pain may be God's wake-up call. I suppose all readers would like to have a friend or a son like Reuven.

There are only three women characters in *The Chosen*. Danny's mother, who has little to say and no more to do than to feed and care for her small family: Reb Saunders, Danny, his nameless sister, and his sickly younger brother Levi, who will have to inherit the responsibility of the leadership of the sect when Danny defects to the secular world beyond it. Danny's sister has been betrothed since childhood and is destined to grow old in the closed Hasidic world, in service to a large family of her own. Mr. Malter, a widower, employs a Russian housekeeper, Manya, who cooks and cleans for him and Reuven. That women are so peripheral to the narrative reflects the values of the Orthodox and ultra-Orthodox Jewish communities represented in *The Chosen*. Although Potok does not overtly criticize the patriarchies of the Hasidic family, a reader today cannot but help infer criticism of the marginal role of women in that ultra-religious world, particularly when the reader learns that during worship in the synagogue women are kept behind a curtain of cheesecloth and restricted to a small, rear section of the room.

THEMATIC ISSUES

The great external theme of *The Chosen* is the aftermath of the Holocaust, its impact on Jewish America, and its importance as a prelude to the founding of the State of Israel. Much of the last third of the story reflects the struggle over Zionism in the Jewish community as well as the struggle of Zionists worldwide to establish the new state. The conflict over loyalties engaged in by American Jews is manifested by Potok in the dispute between David Malter and Reb Saunders. It is foreshadowed by the fateful softball game at the novel's beginning.

A second theme that is also external to the story, but not as far off as the Holocaust, is the theme of the American Dream. Sheldon Grebstein points out that "*The Chosen* can be interpreted . . . as an assertion of peculiarly American optimism and social idealism" (25). Danny and Reuven are the children of immigrants, but they have obtained excellent educations. Both youths have fathers who are brilliant men and fine teachers in their individual ways. The young men take for granted that they have occupational choice, that they will have bright futures as long as they are willing to work as hard in the world as they have done in school. They assume that there will be equal opportunity for them. If they think at all about encountering discrimination, they are confident they can overcome it. Lastly, they are unaware of the uniqueness of American opportunity for Jews and other minorities because they never compare their lives with those Jewish youths of their generation who had the misfortune of living in Europe. It is not an exaggeration to state that Potok was consciously writing a very American story.

The third and perhaps the most significant theme in *The Chosen* is that of father-son conflict. The father and son in conflict are Danny and Reb Saunders. The struggle is nonviolent and mainly fought out on the psychological battlefield. Saunders wants his brilliant son to succeed him as leader of his Hasidic sect. He tries to restrict Danny's reading to religious tomes. He fears that his son will fall victim to acculturation by the Gentile world. He is intimidating and controls by the mere implied threat of disapproval. He inflicts knowledge trials on his son. Furthermore, the power of the community and the weight of ancient tradition serve his will.

His father's attempted mind control makes Danny physically ill and depressed, but Danny is already "infected" by Western knowledge and culture as well as American secularism. The prize to be won by Danny is worth fighting for, even against his father. That prize is freedom— freedom of choice, freedom of action, freedom of thought, and freedom of intellectual inquiry. In the end, in the fashion of comedy (here meaning not tragic), the son wins, as is most natural. It is the way of the world, and it is necessary for the change that is the constant product of the succession of generations. The father-son conflict in *The Chosen* is a microcosm of intrafamily struggles between generations of Jewish boys rejecting the values and strictures of their fathers, only in many cases to return to at least some of them when they are fathers themselves.

STYLISTIC AND LITERARY DEVICES

The description of the world of New York City Hasidism is fascinating to the reading public, both Gentile and Jewish. Potok has excellent descriptive powers, and his portrayal of the seemingly exotic community and its environs is like a travelogue to a foreign land inhabited by a very different people. This is not only the experience of the reader; it is the same for the point-of-view character/narrator, Reuven. The accuracy, detail, and richness of Potok's re-creation of a specific community at a certain time is one of the major achievements of *The Chosen*. One could also compare aspects of the novel to a documentary film depicting a society radically different from mainstream America. A camera eye seems to roam the streets and enter into homes and the synagogue with Reuven. The documentary quality is emphasized by the frequent interjections of background "essays" on the historical evolution as well as the customs of the Hasidic community.

Potok's decision to use a first-person narrative for the telling of the story works particularly well. Reuven is appealing as a personality, and he is easy to identify with for young people. This technique fits very well with Potok's role as teacher/writer as does his use of interspersed documentation in the form of history or sociology lectures. The latter, for some readers, however, may prove to be somewhat off-putting or delaying of the narrative flow. Nevertheless, the serious reader should slow down and absorb the lessons. There is much to be learned from Chaim Potok.

Special note must be made of Potok's brilliant use of eye imagery in the novel. Eye/eyes/eyeglasses stand for seeing, opening up of vision, recognition, and so on. At the beginning of the novel, as the ball game has commenced, Reuven keeps pushing up his glasses on the bridge of his nose so that they won't fall off during an important play (15). This description establishes Reuven as a serious student, a reader, but also it foreshadows the accident to his eye that will happen shortly when it is struck by a piece of eyeglass. Glasses are both a way of seeing better and a barrier to the world. The glasses are broken. The sliver that enters his eye symbolically opens his eyes to the Hasidic world of his friend-to-be.

Danny's repentant visit to Reuven in the hospital is the beginning not only of friendship but also of Reuven's comprehension of the traditions and values of the Hasidic community that he and his friends have disparaged. Also, the suffering that Reuven endures because of his eye injury makes him more understanding of the suffering of others, starting with fellow patients on the eye ward of the hospital. It is a maturing factor. Reuven is very aware, as his eye slowly heals, of darkness and light, as when he leaves his father's dark study and enters the bright living room (100–102). When Danny is learning about earlier Jewish history, he recognizes that people are complicated because they are blind to themselves; that is, they lack insight (156).

As Danny comes to "see" more and more of the outside world his eyes begin to blink and tire (182, 184). Finally, as the young men have matured to their full height and have begun to grow facial hair, Danny is wearing glasses (203). Discovering the secular world that he finds so fascinating now requires the assistance of another set of eyes so to speak. This is surely an experience many young people have as they attack the mountains of printed material or Web sites they have been attracted to or required to read.

But eyes have other functions besides seeing. When Danny is forbidden to speak to Reuven, they communicate with their eyes (252). The final eye reference in the novel is on the last page when Danny's eyes glow as he realizes that he soon will be studying at Columbia University where there will be so much more of the world to "see" (284).

A PSYCHOANALYTIC READING OF *THE CHOSEN*

What Is Psychoanalytic Theory?

Psychoanalytic theory is a method of understanding and explaining the production of literary works and their effects on readers, based on the psychological insights and doctrines of Sigmund Freud, a Viennese Jewish physician and psychoanalyst. Freud identified the unconscious as a major and influential source of psychic energy to the extent that the unconscious strongly influences conscious behavior. Then he created a model that explained the psychological sources of human behavior and a vocabulary that interpreted the model.

The psyche has three parts. First there is the *id* or "it": unconscious, primitive, driving to fulfill basic needs. It is the mind as demanding infant. Then there is the *ego* or "I": conscious, orderly, rational. The *ego* projects itself into the world through the *superego*: conscience, value signifying, judgmental, self-regulating. The *superego* is a product of the influence of upbringing and societal environment on the ego. It respects the reality principle, the denial of immediate pleasure to avoid unpleasant consequences, allowing for later gratification. The conscious mind loads the unconscious mind with thoughts or instincts that must be censored and repressed. They are often of a sexual nature. These repressions return to consciousness in disguises such as creative activity, dreams, or language accidents (Freudian slips). This schematic of the mind as personality has attracted both writers and critics from the beginning of the twentieth century.

The latest major disciple of Freud is the French structuralist Jacques Lacan, who sees the unconscious as a language and thus dreams as a form of discourse like a short story or a novel. Therefore the study of literature should be like the interpretation of dreams: examining symbols; discovering suppressed, sometimes Oedipal (from Sophocles' dramatic hero Oedipus who inadvertently murdered his father and married his mother) sexual longings and drives; learning how emotions are displaced onto neutral or inappropriate objects; recognizing contradictions and condensations of ideas or emotions; and deconstructing language for the hidden or opposite meanings. In other words literary criticism psychoanalyzes the text and the author. It seeks the underlying meaning of the work and probes the reasons for and methods of production.

Although original Freudian theory is less popular and more frequently criticized today than in the past, there is still much to learn about the production and consumption (reading) of fiction from post-Freudian psychoanalytic theory.

The Reading

Since the novel's focus is on Danny Saunders, and since the central conflict of the novel, at least on the personal level, is the father-son conflict between Danny and Reb Saunders, it is most productive to read and discuss that element of the novel in Freudian terms. The unconscious desire of the male child is to displace the father in the mother's affection. It is interesting to note that because Reuven's mother is dead, he cannot have such a desire and thus his relationship with his father is made infinitely easier than Danny's with his father. Danny's mother is almost a nonentity in the novel, and thus a reader might conclude that the author's unconscious dictated the neutralization or elimination of the mother as a means of facilitating peace between fathers and sons—and even within male society when male fraternal bonding is based on the putting down of women.

Danny's enemy is not only his father but his own superego because he was born into such a rigid community. It demands that he be sacrificed, in a kind of scapegoating, to the community's need for a smooth succession to, or reincarnation of, their Godlike father-figure ruler. Thus Reb Saunders's desires are greatly reinforced by community pressure.

But Danny lives in America, a country born in rebellion against a father figure, and thus his connection with the more Americanized or secularized Malters is his lifeline out of his Oedipal bondage. The shaving of the sidelocks (note the word "locks") is the striking off of chains and his "voyage" by subway to Columbia University is his voyage of discovery to his New World. Even his earlier reading of Freud in German, the language then of the mortal enemies of the Jews, is an unconscious double act of aggressive rebellion and revenge against his father that Reuven senses but Danny disavows. Danny has struck out because his father has tried to objectify him, to make him into a clever, parroting, pliant creature without feelings.

Fortunately, and somewhat difficult to accept in the novel, Reb Saunders capitulates rather easily at the end, and so, metaphorically speaking, no blood is shed. Saunders does not mourn for his "lost" son in the traditional Orthodox and ultra-Orthodox Jewish way by saying the prayer for the dead and *cutting off* the son from further communication by shunning.

In Freudian Oedipal theory the male child fears that his rival, his father, will castrate him (turn him into a woman) if he suspects the competition, so the child represses the feeling especially when his superego informs him that the desire for his mother is "unnatural" and thus a taboo. So the repressed antagonism emerges to consciousness in Danny's case with his rebellion against his father's desire to make him the successor to his leadership of the congregation. Most significantly, it is Danny's reading of Freud that provides much of the ammunition for his successful revolt against and defeat of his father, who, unconsciously, may be trying to deprive Danny of his individual manhood by turning him into a clone of himself.

Danny's avid study of Freud is akin to his voracious study of the Talmud. He almost makes Freud into a fatherly priest and the psychoanalyst's writing into a secular religion (Abramson, 18). Potok has Reb Saunders buy into that concept when he states that Danny may yet be a tzaddik (a saintly person) when he becomes a psychologist (280). Freudian theory is set up as a quasi-religion and then rejected when Danny opts for a more "scientific" approach to psychology.

Psychoanalytic assumptions may say as much about the critic who makes them as they do about the writer under scrutiny or the narrative being analyzed. The popular appeal of *The Chosen*, however, may reside in the portrayal of some of the contradictory binary passions that conflict within our individual and collective unconscious: belief and skepticism, feeling and thinking, heart and head, obeying and confronting what Lacan calls "the law of the father," challenging or conforming, building or breaking, or in terms of the novel, being both a Reuven and a Danny.

4

The Promise
(1969)

Hugh Nissenson wrote in the *New York Times Book Review: "The Chosen* established Chaim Potok's reputation as a significant writer. *The Promise* re-affirms it. It is a better book. . . . Potok has demonstrated his ability to deal with a more complex conception and to suffuse it with pertinence and vitality. His promise is fulfilled" (21). Not every critic would agree with this statement, but it is clear that Potok's continuation of the story of Danny Saunders and Reuven Malter's growing up indicates Potok's further maturation as a serious American novelist.

The Promise is more complex than *The Chosen*. It is a novel of teachers and ideas. It is also a novel about students and study. Reuven Malter is studying at an Orthodox Yeshiva toward ordination as a rabbi. His girl-friend, later Danny Saunders's wife, Rachel Gordon, is an English major studying for her bachelor of arts degree. And Danny is working toward a Ph.D. in clinical psychology at Columbia University while preparing for the rabbinate on the side. In studying and preparing for their professions the promising young men meet unexpected challenges.

Reuven, made more liberal by his father's brilliant scholarship in his study and interpretation of the Talmud, confronts a teacher who will do almost anything to destroy the new, scientific method of hermeneutics (defining principles of interpretation of holy texts), even to denying rabbinical ordination to his brightest student. And Danny, studying for a Ph.D. in psychology at Columbia University, combats pessimistic, conventional psychiatric treatment when he draws on his childhood experience and his intuition to propose an unorthodox treatment with which he saves a young man from life in a mental institution or possible self-destruction.

The title, *The Promise*, refers to the promise God made to Abraham in Genesis that the Jewish people would be blessed among nations. In exchange they must promise that they will forever unquestioningly worship God alone. In one of the epigraphs to *The Promise* Potok quotes the nineteenth-century Rebbe of Kotzke who said to God: "Send us our Messiah, for we have no more strength to suffer.... Otherwise ... I rebel against Thee. If thou dost not keep Thy Covenant, then neither will I keep that Promise, and it is all over, we are through being Thy chosen people." The Jewish scholars in *The Promise*—European Orthodox, American Orthodox, and liberal Conservative—vigorously dispute the way to keep the Jewish part of the bargain with God.

Thus *The Promise* is a novel about taking chances—gambling, in a sense. Hugh Nissenson says that the gamble is part of the human condition (5). For thousands of years the Jews, a people with high moral and ethical standards codified into law, have been gambling their very existence on God's promise. Potok opens the novel with a scene of gambling at a country carnival where a game is rigged against three young Jewish people: Reuven; Rachel, his girlfriend at the time; and Michael, her mentally unstable fifteen-year-old cousin. They cannot win regardless of the choices they make.

Later, Reuven will have to choose between standing up for his father and possibly not being ordained as a rabbi, or losing his integrity but achieving the career goal he has been working towards for years. Danny must gamble with his career as a psychologist in order to save his patient and justify his abandonment of Hasidic leadership. Rachel will have to choose between giving up Danny, the young man she comes to love and who wants to marry her, or joining him in a Hasidic life that not only is alien to her but is also a life of difficult restrictions. Truly, choices are the stepping-stones of every life. And each stretching step is a risk, a danger.

Book One's epigraph is a quote from the seventeenth-century French philosopher Pascal that seems to speak to the young people in the book and to the Jewish people in general: "Yes, but you must wager. It is not optional. You are embarked."

The Promise is also a novel about the growth to adulthood, the assuming of independence and authority of admirable young men who will contribute much to society. In it, as is the way of the world, the sons grow taller as their fathers shrink. Moreover, *The Promise* is a book that can help young people find the courage to overcome the outdated impediments of culture and tradition from a moribund past.

The scenes of the novel include the Brooklyn settings in *The Chosen*, other parts of Brooklyn and Manhattan, and the summer resort area near Peekskill, New York, in the Catskill Mountains. Again Potok chooses a first-person narrative. Reuven tells the story once more, but this time he is more central than Danny.

PLOT DEVELOPMENT

The Promise is divided into a prologue and three books. Books One and Three have four chapters each and Book Two has eight. Book One opens with a long, sensational episode that sets two of the main themes of the novel: the need for young people to make difficult choices and the conflict between Orthodox European Jews who have survived the Holocaust and less Orthodox, more humanistic American Jews who sympathize with the survivors but believe that their religion must not founder on rigid religiosity.

Reuven, Rachel, and her cousin Michael are spending part of the summer in the Catskills—Reuven with his father and Rachel with her parents, both of whom are college professors. Michael is also staying with Rachel's family while his parents, Abraham and Ruth Gordon, a liberal rabbinical scholar and his research assistant, are visiting Israel. The young people set out in Rachel's parents' car to what they think is a country fair but turns out to be a seedy carnival. Neither Rachel nor Reuven likes carnivals and neither wants to stay, but Michael, who seems spoiled and neurotic, insists. Reluctantly they let him have his way, a decision they will regret as he causes continual trouble.

Finally, they end up at a game of chance that both Rachel and Reuven know better than to get involved with, but again, Michael is insistent. Frenetically he attempts to win a radio he'd like to give his parents upon their return, and he is suckered into wagering more and more of his money. When that has been lost he cajoles a loan from Reuven. The older youths are appalled at Michael's obsessive-compulsive behavior, but to placate the distraught boy, the ever kind and considerate Reuven lets Michael use all of his money in the wagering.

The owner of the carnival game appears, and he turns out to be an old Jewish man who says he is a concentration camp survivor. He says that he will "take care" of these nice Jewish kids. Instead, he does the final cheating, and Michael cracks up, shouting that the old man hated "us." Later we will realize that unconsciously he means his father and himself. He has identified in his mind the conniving old man with the Orthodox scholars who have spewed hatred on his father. We also learn later that he thinks his fellow yeshiva students hate him too because of his father's writing. Michael threatens the vicious old man, but Reuven prevents violence, leading Michael away from the hateful confrontation.

Michael, whose nose is bleeding in reaction to his stress, is almost out of his mind. Rachel and Reuven get him to her summer place where her parents are angry with the young couple for letting him play the foolish game. Michael then disappears from his room and Reuven searches for him, fearing that the disturbed boy might hurt himself but Michael is only stargazing. He is very knowledgeable in astronomy. Studying the heavens calms him.

Previously Reuven has told Rachel about his best friend, Danny Saunders, and she is very interested in meeting Danny. She reminds Reuven that he was going to invite Danny to visit the next week. Her interest seems stronger than merely being curious about her boyfriend's pal.

The next day Reuven is still shaken by the experience with Michael. Rachel phones him, and we learn that she, an English major in college, is working on a term paper on James Joyce's great Irish novel *Ulysses*, based in part on Homer's *The Odyssey*. References to Joyce and *Ulysses* continue and build throughout *The Promise*. The chapter of *Ulysses* called "Ithaca" comes to be the one Rachel is most interested in, because in part it is about how two people from very different cultural backgrounds become close and caring. Rachel will turn from her friendship with Reuven to deep love for Danny the Hasid. She finds in "Ithaca" a model of acceptance of extreme difference that will aid her eventual embracing of the Hasidic way of life later as Danny's bride.

The ever compassionate Reuven, a rabbi-to-be, is concerned about Michael, and he offers to take the younger youth sailing. Reuven is adept at sailing small boats. Michael knows little about sailing but is willing to learn. They sail together and Michael enjoys the experience and the chance to be distracted from his psychological suffering. They heave to in a cove, and like Huckleberry Finn and Jim, they swim, lie about, talk, and see shapes in the clouds. The clouds are like a giant Rorschach test through which Michael symbolically relates to Reuven the nature of his suffering. A psychotic, he has wide mood swings—ups and downs that are like riding a roller coaster. And he was traumatized by the carnival event that connected him to the hatred many Orthodox Jewish men have for his father and Orthodox Jewish students in his yeshiva have for him because he shares his father's surname: Gordon.

Michael knows of one old Orthodox scholar who has been particularly hateful toward his father, one Rav Kalman who teaches at Hirsch College, Reuven's school. Kalman is Reuven's Talmud teacher. Talmud is the most important subject in the curriculum for rabbinical ordination. In fact, Reuven cannot become a rabbi through his college without the consent of Kalman, who not only hates Michael's father but will come to hate Reuven's too. It is this shared vulnerability to the rigidity and McCarthy-like tactics of Kalman that causes Michael to bond with Reuven, trusting him and desiring his friendship. Michael is suffering, among other things, from Jewish self-hatred manifested by his intolerance toward those who vehemently disagree with his father's theological research.

Soon Abraham Gordon phones the Malter house, tests Reuven's knowledge of Talmud, which is outstanding, and conveys greetings from Michael. Gordon wants to encourage the Michael-Reuven friendship. When Rachel calls Reuven she is interested only in learning if Danny is really coming although Reuven is even willing to talk about James Joyce.

Danny, who is living in a tiny, dingy apartment near Columbia University, has been delayed. He is doing his pre-doctoral field work and is tied up with emergency patients but is coming soon. When Reuven visits his friend he is appalled at the unsanitary mess, and he forces open a window to air the place out, but the pale, gaunt glasses-wearing graduate student is still Hasid enough to prefer the enclosed world of books, ideas, and argument to the natural world. Reuven tells him that he needs a girl. Perhaps Reuven is already thinking of "giving" his best friend Rachel, for Reuven seems to have little interest in females although he does comment on the fact that Ruth Gordon and Rachel's mother are beautiful women.

Professor Gordon reveals to Reuven upon first meeting him that Michael has been in therapy three times but to no avail. A major suspense element of the novel is not knowing the reason for Michael's disfunctioning. It comes out at the end in the novel's most dramatic scene. Rachel's father and Reuven arrange for Michael to be out when Danny visits and talks with Michael's father. After Danny arrives at Reuven's place Rachel takes him to her house. The reader assumes that a relationship is about to begin with a short trip in a car. When Rachel returns

Danny after his meeting with the Gordons, Rachel has only a nod and
a "pale smile" for Reuven before driving off. From Danny, Reuven learns
how sick Michael is. He burns books. He behaves badly in school. He
has smashed his beloved telescope. The Gordons are worried and frightened over their mentally deteriorating son. Danny will try to get Michael
into the Robert H. Selby Residential Treatment Center for Children in
which he is interning.

Meanwhile Rachel and Reuven meet one evening and swim off a dock.
She asks again for information about Danny. And they confess to each
other that their relationship is simply as good "friends." The suspense
as to whether or not Rachel and Reuven will love each other is over, and
now the slight romantic interest in the novel shifts to whether Danny
will respond to Rachel's apparent interest and, if so, whether or not they
can overcome the cultural gulf between them.

Reuven and his father return to their apartment in Williamsburg,
Brooklyn, and Reuven goes back to college. He learns that Michael has
been admitted to the residential treatment center after resisting and be-
having hysterically. But Danny has won the confidence of Michael because he is Reuven's best friend, and so Michael accepts the situation
and settles down. Danny is going to treat him under the supervision of
a senior psychologist.

Rachel meanwhile is trying to learn as much about Hasidism as she
can, and Reuven is helping his father by reading proofs for him at the
Frankel library in the school where Professor Gordon works. Most of
Reuven's day is spent in the study of Talmud for Rav Kalman's class,
but Reuven, who dislikes Rav Kalman, will have nothing to do with his
teacher socially. Kalman is the worst kind of teacher: unwilling to answer
questions, "angry, impatient, sarcastic," and without humor.

Still Reuven is fascinated by the opinionated, bigoted man, for besides
being a brilliant if traditional Talmud scholar he has an interesting history and is a Holocaust survivor. When Rav Kalman learns that Reuven
has been visiting the Zechariah Frankel Library and that he knows Abraham Gordon, he makes Reuven's life miserable by taunting and tor-
menting him in and out of class. He orders Reuven not to enter the
Frankel school again under threat of refusing his ordination. Other students at Hirsch College are so intimidated that they begin to shun Reuven. Kalman has infected the school with suspicion, rancor, and fear.
This is McCarthyism in a school at the time it is occurring in the nation.

Late one night Michael makes a surreptitious phone call to Reuven
and begs him to come and visit him in the treatment center. Reuven is

in a dilemma because Danny's supervisor in the case, for whom Michael has no respect, does not want Reuven to visit the patient. Still he promises to visit. But first, because of his father's urging, Reuven goes to Danny to see if it is all right to visit Michael. Over coffee they first talk about Rachel. Danny finds it hard to do so, but Reuven lets him know that he is not hurt.

Actually, it is Michael and his deteriorating condition that is foremost on Danny's mind. The treatment is not working, and something else must be tried. Michael is not cooperating, and he is causing trouble with other patients. Also he has burned a Bible his father gave him and has revealed sex fantasies about Rachel. Danny and his supervisor have no notion about what is really bothering Michael, and if they can't get through to him he will have to be placed in a secure institution. Reuven, ever intuitive, senses that Danny is planning to use isolation and solitude on Michael to break him down and open up his inner feelings. It is what Danny's father, Reb Saunders, used to sensitize him.

But Danny is afraid that such a radical treatment might not work and might cause Michael to grow more psychotic. Yet Danny, a Freudian, is committed to the talking cure, and so Michael must reveal his painful, unconscious repression to be made well again. It is the early 1950s and safe psychotropic medications are little known or not trusted.

Meanwhile Reuven is only four months from his ordination exams, and he must walk on eggs to avoid a disastrous encounter with Rav Kalman. But his father's new book is out, and if he does not choose to interpret the Talmud in the traditional European way, never questioning the validity and accuracy of the text, he will not pass his "semicha," his ordination examination.

Reuven visits Michael at the Selby Treatment Center. They walk on the grounds and come to a pagodalike gazebo in the garden. Michael calls it his house and states that he will live in it one day soon with Rachel. Michael is clearly worse. His sorrowful parents arrive, and they invite Reuven to dinner as they want to talk to him about Michael and about Danny. Michael very much wants Reuven to accept. Reuven seems to be a lifeline for him, a rope to sanity. Reuven has to choose between helping his young friend and the Gordons and risking the vengeance of Rav Kalman who has prohibited further contact with Abraham Gordon. He chooses to help Michael. And he will not deny his father's scholarship even if he loses his chance to be a rabbi.

Rav Kalman's article attacking David Malter's book appears, and Danny thinks that it is an honest piece. Reuven is angry that Rav Kalman used him to prepare the basis for his attack on his father's book. Reb Saunders takes an interest in Danny's patient, but he is more interested in the relationship between his son and the young woman who is a Gordon and a niece of the man he thinks is an apostate. But Reb Saunders's worries are assuaged when he learns that all the Gordons "observe the Commandments." He still cannot be open enough with his son to ask him about the young woman he has been seeing.

The Kalman article is causing trouble for David Malter in the yeshiva where he has taught for many years. He may have to resign even though he has tenure because he could not work effectively in a hostile atmosphere. So Reuven's ordination is in doubt, and his father seems ready to give up his job because of the rigidity and intolerance of a teacher.

On his second visit to Michael, Reuven is taken by the disturbed youth to the pagoda again where Michael says that Rachel is inside. Knowing that Reuven is suffering over the mistreatment by Rav Kalman, Michael wonders why Reuven doesn't leave the "spiders and cobwebs and old men who cheat you" (208). When Reuven is distracted for a moment, Michael runs off and tries to set the pagoda on fire because he does not like the way the pagoda, "his house," has been painted. Also, a fire would warm up his chilled friend Reuven, who has rushed back to the pagoda and who scuffles with Michael to prevent him from lighting a pile of leaves. Michael is led back to his room and Danny is phoned. In the room Danny begins to get Michael to talk but at crucial times he resists further inquiry.

Reuven realizes that the pagoda is painted the same color as the gaming booth where they were cheated last summer. Danny is convinced that Michael is terrified of his own rage, fearing that he will hurt other people. Danny is now convinced that an extended period of isolation in total silence would make Michael so hungry for talk that he would drop his resistance and open up to analysis. Being disorganized over a long period hopefully would result in regression and that would permit Michael to rebuild his ego, his presence in the real world. Michael will be locked in a room without furniture, given food and drink of course, but no conversation.

Further complicating things is that Rachel inadvertently indicated to Michael that she and Danny have a relationship, and now he is angry with his therapist. Michael is extremely dangerous. He is filled with aggression, fear, anger, and hostility. He organizes an armed breakout of the treatment center by leading some other disturbed youths to break into the kitchen, steal knives, threaten a guard, and almost get away.

Michael is trapped in the pagoda, and Danny bravely takes the knife out of the hand of this boy who wants to kill him for seeming to take Reuven and Rachel away from him.

Reuven is shaken. He turns his thoughts inward and realizes to his astonishment that he has anger too. He is angry with his saintly father for the book he has written and the limited life he has allowed both of them.

The repressed hatred of Michael for his father is destroying him. With the consent of his parents, Michael is brought into a small room in the treatment center and told that he will be left alone for a short time. He fights the attendants and is locked in screaming and raging. Weeks go by and Michael haunts Reuven's dreams. Rachel has met Danny's father and the reception was cool. Reb Saunders reacted as if Rachel and her parents were stealing Danny from him and Hasidism. Although she is deeply in love with Danny and plans on marriage in June, when she will be graduated from college, she confides to Reuven her misgivings about the relationship with a man who out of religious principles does not touch her or take her hand, and who asked on their second date if she was a virgin. Reuven, ever the good friend, assures her that Danny will never hurt her and should be trusted. Now Reuven won't even let the grateful Rachel kiss him on his cheek (276).

A favorable but temporary reversal of fortune occurs for David Malter. He plans to give up his yeshiva job because of the controversy his book has caused. To his surprise, Reuven's school, Hirsch College, has approached him about an appointment in the graduate department the school is planning. Hirsch College is now Hirsch University. Reuven is overjoyed but the university has to deal with the powerful Rav Kalman. In a moment of truthful conversation Reuven tells Kalman that he has read Gordon's books but has not been influenced by them. Reuven has come to realize that there is a wall between him and Abraham Gordon. Gordon loves the Jewish people, is full of brilliant ideas, is fully committed to the truth, and is a good human being—what Jews call a "mensch"—but he does not believe in God. Reuven does. He still is an Orthodox Jew. Yet he will not give up the right to read, to inquire, to seek answers in books.

Danny enters. The clever Abraham Gordon has phoned him and urged him to come to his friend's defense. The young Talmudic genius takes over the conversation, for Rav Kalman has awe and respect for the brilliant son of Reb Saunders, a young man who had become a rabbi a year and a half ago while also studying for his Ph.D. Wilting under Danny's intellectual reasoning and upon learning that Gordon's son is very ill and Reuven is involved in the treatment, Rav Kalman lifts the ban on Reuven's seeing Gordon. All he now asks of his student is that he does not become a "goy" (Gentile). By goy, of course, Rav Kalman means any person who is not an Orthodox or ultra-Orthodox Jew.

But Rav Kalman has set his sights on preventing the establishment of a graduate department at Hirsch in which modern methods of scholarship would be taught. Mr. Malter is not sure he wants to move from one controversial appointment to another. A compromise is worked out at Hirsch between the supporters of Rav Kalman and the liberals. The department will be established but David Malter will not be appointed to a post in it. The saintly Malter does not hate nor blame Rav Kalman, whom he sees as trying desperately to save what little is left of his broken world.

Danny and Reuven have been best friends for seven years and yet their fathers have never met. Rav Saunders refrained from attacking Mr. Malter's book in gratitude for his helping Danny and allowing Reuven to serve as intermediary between him and his son.

Now the two representatives of fatherhood and the pre-World War II generation meet in Reb Saunders's synagogue to celebrate the engagement of Rachel and Danny. Abraham Gordon is there too. The symbolic significance is that there is hope for the unity of the Jewish people, or at least Jewish men. The synagogue is filled only with men. No women are in sight. Rachel, her mother, Danny's mother and sister, and all the other women are in another place celebrating by themselves. When Reb Saunders, Rachel's father Joseph Gordon, and Danny enter, Reb Saunders sees David Malter and he embraces and kisses him.

The time for Reuven's ordination examination is coming, and Rav Kalman demands that the student choose between his father's scientific readings of the Talmud—in which case Kalman will not give him the exam—or Kalman's rigid, closed-minded traditionalism. But Reuven refuses to choose and says he can only demonstrate his position at the exam. Therefore, it is Rav Kalman who must choose either to give the bright young man a chance or ruin his life unjustly, without a fair hearing. Kalman gives in. Reuven gets his examination.

Finally, in chapter 15, the long suspense over whether or not Reuven will become a rabbi is resolved. Rav Kalman has consented to the oral semicha examinations, and there are three days of them. Reuven honestly answers the interrogations by Kalman and his antagonist, the liberal teacher Rabbi Gershenson. Most of the questions concern interpretations of the Talmud. Reuven is not afraid to say where he thinks the ancient scribes erred because they did not have the most accurate source text available. Reuven's knowledge is unassailable, and to the examiners' amazement the source of key information came from the Frankel Seminary Library. His analysis is brilliant but threatening to the old line. If he taught this way a revolution in Talmud teaching might occur. A frozen text would be thawed out.

Wisely and out of deep conviction Reuven draws a fine line. He will teach Talmud using comparative texts and external sources but he will *not* teach the Pentateuch, that is, the Torah, the most sacred part of the Jewish Bible, that way. The Five Books of Moses were received by the Jewish people directly from God. The exam is concluded and Reuven must wait days for the result. Meanwhile, the tense Reuven receives the happy news that his father has accepted a position as a professor of Talmud at the Zechariah Frankel Seminary. Malter was leaving the yeshiva he had helped to create. His decision symbolizes the changing world of Judaism. There is a polarization between Orthodox rabbis, locked into traditional interpretations and practices, and the community Orthodox rabbis serve. That lay community is less and less willing to support the inaccurate, the improbable, and the inflexible.

Through his scholarship and because of the rigidity and viciousness of the attack on his book, Malter has moved into a more liberal camp of Judaism, the Conservative. The suspense of the struggle between David Malter and Rav Kalman over the soul of Judaism, symbolically sited in that bright representative of the next generation of Jewish leaders, Reuven Malter, is over and has resulted in somewhat of a draw. Rav Kalman has kept Mr. Malter from Hirsch, but Malter has landed a prestigious post at Frankel, and his son will stay on at Hirsch carrying the banner of modern scholarly inquiry. Finally Rav Kalman calls Reuven to tell him that he will be given semicha; he will be a rabbi after all.

Later, Rav Kalman explains to Reuven that he did not want to pass him, but he did not want to drive him away from the school. Also he now has a little sympathy for Malter's scholarly method, having heard it through a human voice, a voice that gave it life. He will fight Reuven in print and in the class, but it will be for the sake of the Torah and not personal. There has been a compromise, however. The brilliant Reuven is never to teach Talmud in the rabbinical school where future rabbis are instructed, but he is offered an appointment in the new graduate department of rabbinics. Rav Kalman, having just ordained Rabbi Malter, could not object. To his father's triumphant delight, Rabbi Malter accepts.

As the months pass Michael's condition remains unchanged. He is docile, silent, without emotions. Danny expected this but not for such a long period and has begun to doubt his method. Michael's parents begin to disagree on whether to continue the treatment. Ruth Gordon wants it stopped, but Abraham insists that it must be seen through.

The climax to the Michael plot comes in chapter 16, the last. It is the most dramatic scene in the novel, as if it had been written with a film in mind. Danny, Reuven, and the Gordons enter the tiny, dimly lit room in which Michael has been incarcerated. He is thin, limp, and without expression. At first he does not answer Reuven's questions, and Reuven fears that they have killed his spirit and his soul. He panics and begins to say what comes to mind: praising Michael's sailing skills, talking about the ordination exam and his teaching job, and shouting that he took on his adversaries and won and that Michael must fight too.

Finally Michael responds: "You're getting semicha from Rav Kalman?" (352). Michael continues to question his friend and grows angry because he feels that Reuven was a traitor to accept semicha from Rav Kalman. Danny jumps in and explains that Reuven learned from his father, Reb Saunders, what he used to win out over the old man, and then he asks the key question: "Would you have wanted Reuven not to have gotten semicha and to hate his father?" (354). He pushes beyond the question to ask if Michael wanted Reuven to fail so that he would come to be like Michael and they could share secrets. Those as yet unspoken secrets are blurted out in a cathartic flow of words erupting from Michael's mouth. He hates his religion because his experiences have caused him to see it as one that makes people hate other people. And he both hates and loves his father. He hates him because they share the name that has been attacked.

In Michael's case a key source of the poison is his father's scrapbook of negative criticism. Michael hates those who hate his father and him, but he also hates his fellow victim, his father. Yet his father is a good, loving parent and he knows that too, and so he is impaled on the contradistinctions in his unconscious mind: he loves and hates his father. And he loves and hates his mother for she has helped his father write the books that have caused his misery. And he loves and hates the religion that is both a torment and a solace. He screams: "I hate you!" at his parents (358) and falls into their open arms shouting the healing, forgiving words addressed to his religion as well as his mother and father: "Oh God, I love you so much!" (358). The crisis has passed and poor, suffering Michael is on his way to a normal life through more psychoanalysis.

Danny and Rachel are married. She will go to graduate school at Columbia while Danny finishes his Ph.D. As the novel ends Danny, Rachel, the Gordons, and the Malters are back in the Catskills in August, and Danny goes sailing with Michael who when he now looks at the clouds sees . . . clouds.

HISTORICAL BACKGROUND

The novel is set in the early 1950s. Its background is the beginning of the longest conflict of the twentieth century, the cold war between the Soviet Union and the United States of America. The opening event of the war was the Berlin Blockade by the Soviets in 1948. As the events of *The Promise* unfold, the Korean War, which began in 1950, is underway. American and South Korean troops are fighting North Korean and Chinese Communist armies. But unlike World War II, the Korean War seems far from the consciousness of Reuven and the other characters in the novel.

But the aftermath of World War II does impact on Reuven and his father. For one, the section of Williamsburg in which the Malters live seems to Reuven to be filling up with Hasidic survivors of the concentration camps. Gentiles seem to have disappeared (*The Promise*, 1). Reuven, despite his sympathy for his coreligionists, appears apprehensive about their presence in overwhelming numbers (Woodman, 41). In this regard *The Promise* is a darker novel, "more pensive and less comforting" (Bandler, 13) than *The Chosen*. In the latter the Hasidic community as seen through Reuven's ingenuous eyes has a certain warmth and exotic charm. Now, filled out with survivors, the ultra-Orthodox community appears full of intolerance and seems a threat to intellectual freedom so important to American thought.

Fascism has been defeated and destroyed. The communist threat seems far away, in Asia and Eastern Europe. The threat to Jews in America is the same threat that endangered all Americans, the threat to American democracy in the McCarthy period. Then Senator Joseph McCarthy of Wisconsin, through dishonest, undemocratic, intimidating practices undertaken in the name of anticommunism, but in fact self-serving, threatened the constitutional foundations of the United States. Fortunately, his unethical ways were exposed, and he was disgraced.

Ironically, in *The Promise* Reuven is faced with McCarthy-like treatment in his seminary, when his teacher Rav Kalman, himself a survivor of the greatest evil of the century, uses any method he can to fight what he considers heresy in the interpretation of holy texts. In the end justice prevails in the Jewish community as it did in America. But also, as in American history, there was much individual suffering until the nation learned a painful lesson about the need to be vigilant against unprincipled demagogues or extremists so sure of their rectitude that they will embrace any wickedness to further their ideology. The McCarthy episode, a blot on our democratic history, has left a scar noticeable even today.

CHARACTER DEVELOPMENT

The Promise has more fully developed major characters than *The Chosen*. The two fathers/two sons pattern of the latter is replaced in *The Promise* with a more complicated set of relationships. But there is the same generational divide as in *The Chosen*. The younger generation is represented by the narrator and chief character Reuven Malter; his friend, Danny Saunders, and his younger friend, the psychologically disturbed Michael; and Rachel, the college student who first dates Reuven and then falls in love with Danny and marries him. The older generation is represented by the novel's near villain, Rav Kalman, Reuven's father Mr. Malter, and Abraham Gordon and his wife Ruth.

Reuven Malter remains the fine person we met in *The Chosen*. After all, in *The Promise* he is preparing to become a rabbi. Paradoxically, Reuven, the young man who will earn his living and make his contribution to society as a spiritual leader is, as in *The Chosen*, much more at home in the secular world than his friend Danny Saunders, who will earn his living and make his contribution to society as a clinical psychologist. One of the fine attributes Reuven portrays in *The Chosen* he continues to possess and even enlarge upon. He is a true, loyal, unshakable friend, without guile, and totally reliable. Most important, Reuven stands for the idea that someone can be a humanist and yet remain fully devoted to a religion.

Danny Saunders, a graduate student in psychology at Columbia University, no longer lives in Brooklyn. Instead he has a small apartment near the university. Also, he no longer has a beard and sidelocks. Nor does he wear the black clothes of Hasidic men. But he "remains a Hasid in spirit" (Walden, 235). Furthermore, and not surprisingly, Danny has learned much from his father's extreme ways after all. There is an old expression: "An apple does not fall far from the tree." Despite the fact that Danny is a graduate student in psychology in a modern American university, he goes beyond the conventional in psychiatric treatment and reaches back into the Hasidic tradition to employ his father's ancient technique of using silence to cause an individual to search his or her soul, thus sensitizing it and preparing it for new understanding.

Danny wants very badly to succeed as a clinical psychologist, because he has given up so much and hurt so many in abdicating the leadership role his father and his community trained him for. Also Danny is a competitor and a winner by nature. He undertakes the cure of Michael—at which he works furiously and which is so painful to him—partly because of its challenge. But, having been trained to be a tzaddik—a holy, but more important, a compassionate man—he is equally motivated by his desire to save the mind of a tormented person.

When Danny falls in love with Rachel, he does so constricted by a cultural past he cannot and does not want to change. She must be a virgin, and she must remain so until after marriage. Literally, he will avoid touching any part of her body until then. He cannot bring himself to show public affection. He will expect Rachel to have many children and keep a strictly kosher home. Yet at the end of the novel Rachel is starting a graduate program in English at Columbia, and the reader wonders if Danny may not have to make compromises in the future. The reader expects that he will continue to lighten up under the influence of his wife and his friend.

The greatest change in Danny's personality is that he has lost the hostility that marred his younger days. He has gained, through Reuven's instructive example, the ability to be a true friend. His coming to Reuven's rescue when Rav Kalman is about to disqualify Reuven from the rabbinate is melodramatic: the hero is saved at the last minute by the unexpected arrival of his pal.

Michael Gordon is a very ill young man. He suffers terribly. He is mentally ill because he is torn between hating the father whose liberal publications have caused him to be persecuted and loving his truly caring father and mother. He has Jewish self-hatred because some Orthodox Jews have tormented the Gordons. His fear and repression of this destructive hatred causes his psychological disturbance. All that comes out later, after Danny, the apprentice clinical psychologist, has worked a radical cure on him. Suffering intolerance can have terrible unforeseen consequences in young people, sometimes driving them to desperation. It is Michael's good fortune that through his new friendship with Reuven, Danny Saunders, a most caring healer who is knowledgeable of, if not wedded to Freudian psychoanalysis, will treat him with a dedication and determination that seems almost religious. It is as if both Michael's soul and his Jewish identity are being rescued along with his mind. In the end he is on the way to recovery. He loves and is loved by his parents. He has a good healer and a good older friend. He may have a normal active life and not be locked away in an institution for dangerous mental patients. The talking cure has begun to work.

Rachel Gordon is one of only three women who are in any way prominent in *The Promise*. As Reuven and Danny have matured to young manhood, it seems natural that a novel narrated by a young man would now evidence more awareness of the presence of women. But the world of *The Promise* is very much a man's world even if, unlike *The Chosen*, women are not banished to the kitchen, cemetery, or the back room of a synagogue.

Rachel is an intelligent, sensitive young Jewish college student, privileged in being the child of two college teachers. Through her Reuven meets her troubled cousin Michael. And through Reuven, a young man she likes but does not love, she first hears of Danny. She begins to fantasize about the exotic Hasidic youth who could redirect her assimilated being to her ancient cultural roots. When she meets him she is ready to love him. She is not disappointed. He is attractive and fascinating. And they quickly fall in love, to Reuven's silent dismay. Fortunately Rachel lets Reuven down softly, and we do not feel disappointment in her switching affection, for on her part Reuven was never more than a good friend.

Rachel has many misgivings about "converting" to Hasidism through marriage, but love conquers all. Reservations as to how well she will acclimatize to a lifestyle that seems of another time and another place are set aside.

Rachel is very important for the plot in that she is the connection between the Malters, the Gordons, and the Saunderses. All three young people in *The Promise* share an agenda necessary for their age group and only tenuously connected to the larger community conflicts of the older generation. The young must complete their education and training. They must achieve stability. They must come to understand and in a way "forgive" their parents. And, when appropriate, find their mates.

The only older-generation woman of significance in *The Promise* is Michael's mother, Ruth Gordon. She is a strikingly attractive women, as Reuven notes, and she works as her husband's editorial assistant. She has a Ph.D., presumably in literature, for she has spent a post-doctoral year studying French literature at the great Parisian university, the Sorbonne. She is a linguist, fluent in many languages. Yet she seems content, as were many brilliant and educated women of her generation and class, to spend her life after marriage mothering and homemaking and helping her husband build his career. Although she succeeds as intellectual companion to her husband, she has come close to failing as mother to her son Michael in that somehow his emotional needs have not been understood and met. She has not had the time or chosen to make the time to be both mother and research assistant.

Ruth Gordon is like a Lady Macbeth without the malice. She has directed Abraham Gordon's rabbinical career away from the pulpit and into the world of scholarship. She is a better writer than her husband, so she edits and polishes his work. She seems to get vicarious satisfaction from research and from his publications and growing esteem. Joan Del Fattore notes, "No one in the novel seems to find it remarkable that a woman with a background like Ruth's finds total professional satisfaction in helping in this way with her husband's books" (54). From the perspective of the year 2000, Ruth Gordon's life seems deserving of some pity for the waste of it. The contemporary reader is more interested in her than Potok was in the early 1970s.

The older generation of Jewish men who are of significance in *The Promise* represent the range of political and religious convictions. Judaism is a religion of books, and as most religious Jews believe that the wish and the will of the Deity is revealed through the words in the holy texts, it is of vital importance to be sure, either through faith and tradition and/or scholarship, that the texts are accurate. This is the essence of the religious controversy in *The Promise*. If the texts could be incorrect the interpretations of the sages, past and present, could be wrong. Could they be? Could the ancient scribes have made copy errors? If Judaism is opened by scholarship to differing interpretations, even different facts and procedures, can it still be the same Judaism practiced in Europe for almost two millennia?

On the extreme right—relatively unimportant now in the continuing story of life in the Jewish community of New York City in the first novels of Chaim Potok—is Reb Saunders. The Hasidic community he represents has but little interest in the great debate over the all-important question of reading and authenticating holy texts, for they are totally commited to the belief that the holy texts contain the uncorrupted words of God.

On the far left of a spectrum of Judaism that does not include secular humanists, Abraham Gordon represents the rational, scientific study of

Judaism from the viewpoint of anthropology and sociology. Abraham Gordon is a distinguished and widely published liberal scholar of Judaism as well as a Conservative rabbi whose use of modern biblical scholarship in his theological discourse has made his name an anathema to many on the extreme right of the Orthodox academic world. He has a Ph.D. in philosophy from Harvard and is a professor of Jewish philosophy at the Zechariah Frankel Seminary, a liberal institution. He wants American Judaism to be a religion that appeals to intelligent people who could both love it and respect it.

Although Abraham Gordon is portrayed with great respect for his scholarship and with sympathy for his suffering over Michael, his view of the future direction of Judaism is rejected by all other parties to the great debate: Rav Kalman, Danny, David Malter, and Reuven. One may assume that Potok too, rejects his views. He is intelligent, compassionate, and decent but he is wrong.

Rav Kalman, a hard man, is at the other end of the political/religious spectrum from Abraham Gordon. In some ways he is the most interesting character in the text. Often villains are fascinating especially when they repent or show up in the end as not being all that bad.

Before World War II Rav Kalman had been a teacher in a great Yeshiva in Vilna, Lithuania, and he spent two years in a German concentration camp. Rumors in school reported that German storm troopers had shot to death his wife and three daughters in Poland, and that he escaped from a camp, found his way to Russia, and joined the partisans behind German lines. Another rumor stated that Rav Kalman had hidden out with a Polish family until they were discovered and executed, but he managed to escape to Russia, make his way to Siberia and then to Shanghai, where he remained until the defeat of the Japanese. Then the administration of Hirsch College brought him to America. Rav Kalman has a crippled hand, presumably from torture, but no one is sure. Terrible things have not broken him but rather turned him into steel. He is a sword blade defending the authenticity of all holy texts with indiscriminate swings.

Identifying with Reuven and his plight the reader can hate Kalman, but as the novel progresses the reader may begin to somewhat admire his dogmatism because, unlike Senator Joseph McCarthy, his contemporary prototype, he is not a hypocrite. His crippled hand serves as an emblem of what he has suffered. It serves for us as symbol of his bitterness and inability to care for people as individuals, an inability that is mitigated as the novel progresses. He remains more of a warrior than a docile victim, but now he misperceives as his enemy Jews with more liberal convictions in respect to the authenticity of Jewish religious texts. He will do anything fair or foul to keep alive the values and the traditions of the European Jewry destroyed in the Holocaust.

David Malter represents the middle of the religious/political spectrum of *The Promise*. He has aged since we first met him in Potok's first published novel. As in *The Chosen* he is sometimes ill. His life consists of writing, teaching, and caring for Reuven. One wonders why the widower has not even considered remarriage or a personal relationship with a woman. He has worked hard on his scholarly book, and although it has brought him fame in liberal circles, it has made difficulties for his son just as Gordon's books made difficulties for his. The book has also alienated him from his colleagues in the yeshiva to which he has dedicated his life, especially the outspoken Orthodox new arrivals from Europe. In the end, however, things are well between Reuven and him, and his new position in the academic world of Conservative Judaism bodes well for his future. One cannot help seeing David Malter, like Reuven, as a little too good and too understanding to be true. At least Reuven gets angry sometimes, over religious issues at any rate.

Potok's characters are round, rich, and full. But it is interesting to consider that whereas the significant males—Reuven, Danny, Abraham Gordon, David Malter, Rav Kalman, and Michael Gordon—struggle individually with the profound question of locating themselves within their definition of Jewishness, the significant women—Rachel and Ruth Gordon—are primarily concerned with their relationships with males: lover, husband, son.

THEMATIC ISSUES

The major theme of *The Promise* is the struggle within the Jewish community over what constitutes a good religious Jew. Given that the good Jew obeys the Ten Commandments, the battleground becomes textual. The right wing, people like Rav Kalman and the ultra-Orthodox, insist that the Hebrew Bible and the Talmud, or in other words the Written Law and the Oral Law, are both sacred texts and thus perfect. The left wing, Reconstructionists like Abraham Gordon, consider all religious texts open for correction. Indeed errors and contradictions should be ferreted out and amended through historical processes. The center, people like the Malters, Conservatives and some Orthodox, believe that the

Hebrew Bible is sacred, a received text from God—as do the ultra-Orthodox—but the Talmud has errors and contradictions and is not sacred but open to amendment.

Potok is a centrist, a Conservative, and thus on the side of David and Reuven Malter. Yet these characters and the author never lose their respect for their coreligionists. Thus the ultimate manifestation of this theme of quest for Jewish identity is the hope and possibility of reconciliation and unity within diversity.

Fathers and sons in archetypal conflict, a Freudian theme, is significant in *The Promise*. Michael Gordon's surface hatred for Orthodox Jews, particularly those of the older generation, is a symptom of his illness, not the cause. That is his underlying repressed hatred for his father, who has brought down on both their heads the wrath of those arrogant, hateful people Michael says think themselves above God.

Danny, now a psychologist, has worked out and redirected into his profession his father hatred and so is an excellent therapist for Michael. On the most remote level of his unconscious, Reuven too has father hatred. Watching Michael in therapeutic confession, he comes to understand that, and he is even able, hesitantly, to inform his understanding father, who realizes that Reuven has been suffering psychologically from the torment of Rav Kalman and others brought down on his head by their hatred of the senior Malter and his ideas.

Potok and Freud agree that sons have problems with fathers. Rebellion is natural. When understood, reconciliation comes with maturation. Potok is a strong supporter of what is now called family values. The family portraits in *The Promise* as well as in *The Chosen* are very interesting. The Saunders family is a patriarchy and Danny must outwardly rebel in order to become his own person. He does so successfully in a large measure because his father wisely gives in and sets him free. There will always be tension, but there will always be love between this father and son.

David Malter is much more democratic than Reb Saunders and so Reuven is free from the start, and without a mother for unconscious combat they have the warmest, least inhibited relationship despite the temporary problem of Reuven's seemingly being punished by Orthodoxy for his father's "apostasy," or desertion of his religion. The Gordon family has been hurt because the parents made caring for Michael second to their joint professional career. Thus the process of healing for Michael is concomitant with the healing of the family.

Rav Kalman has lost his family. It is probable that his antagonism to the Malters is in part motivated by unconscious jealousy of David Malter, whose brilliant son lives. The valorizing of the protective, supportive, well-functioning family is an important premise in *The Promise* and in Judaism.

STYLISTIC AND LITERARY DEVICES

In *The Promise* Potok continues to ply his trade and exhibit his skill as a conventional storyteller. For most English language readers *The Chosen* and *The Promise* are cultural excursions, travelogues of the mind, vivid encounters and explorations in the imagination created by the written word. His targeted audience is the mainstream reader, not scholarly critics in universities. The novel has a beginning, a middle, and a clear end. Exposition—that is, establishing time and place and introducing character relationships—is worked in early and appropriately. Most readers of fiction enjoy this kind of comfortable, familiar structure. Potok's goal in *The Promise* and elsewhere is "to explore . . . a certain quadrant of the human experience" (Potok, "The First Eighteen Years," 103).

In *The Promise* Potok continues to use the first-person narrative with Reuven again as the narrator. Reuven is portrayed strongly in *The Chosen*, but he is not the primary focus there. Danny is. Now the audience can enjoy the reacquainting with the likable Reuven and stay with him as he grows into adulthood and faces more worldly challenges than he had to face in *The Chosen*.

Chaim Potok is a student of Ernest Hemingway. He is a minimalist in his dialogue. Often he provides the words, and the reader colors in the emotion. Passages realistically portray portions of speech in the manner of contemporary dramatists like David Mamet and Harold Pinter. For example when Reuven comes to Danny's apartment after their not having seen each other in a long time, and with the mutual knowledge that Rachel is now Danny's girl straining the relationship, Reuven succinctly says:

> "Well . . . how are you?"
> "I'm all right."
> "What have you got that I can thaw out with?"
> "Coffee."
> "Kosher coffee?"
> He smiled.

"It's good to see you," I said.
"Yes," he said quietly. (133)

The tension is palpable. Reuven's joke is as weak as the Columbia grad student's coffee probably is. But it does break the ice, and we can feel the friendship warming up, because between the sparse lines, both parties are expressing complicated feelings and a renewal of affection. The bare "Yes" is affirmation of their earlier brotherly love. The minimal language requires the reader to fill in and thus participate in the narrative.

All realistic narratives imply a future life for their surviving characters, and Potok is quite traditional in this regard. We know pretty much where all are going. But Potok is also able to incorporate serious themes and philosophical discussion without causing too much disruption in the narrative. Readers do not burn out in grappling with religious ideas that may be beyond their cultural experience. Potok achieves this admirable end by attaching philosophical and religious positions to specific characters about whom, to varying degrees, we care.

Symbols are carefully and sparingly employed. In the dark heart of the novel, when all seems despairing, the lighting of the Hanukkah menorah brings light to bear against the enormous darkness of night (226). Michael's sky is his refuge from the painful real world. Michael is always pushing his glasses back up to the bridge of his nose presumably to see better but symbolically to understand more clearly what is perplexing him. Reuven's boat frees Michael and him from the shore, where Michael's dynamic unconscious stews dichotomous hate and love. At the Selby treatment center, prints of boats and models abound because the institute is "off shore" from the world in which Michael must eventually dock safely. Both Danny, the renegade tzaddik, and Abraham Gordon, the "emancipated" intellectual, tug at ears and imaginary sidelocks, for they are not truly free of their religious background, nor, on the unconscious level, do they want to be. Church bells ring when Rav Kalman is about to teach, reminding him and the students that they are a minority in an alien world always ready to intrude on theirs.

A PSYCHOANALYTIC READING OF *THE PROMISE*

Although a psychoanalytic reading of a work of literature is very subjective to the perspective of the reader, it is blatantly obvious that Potok had Freud and psychoanalysis very much in mind when writing *The Promise* as well as, to a lesser extent, *The Chosen*. After all, a major plot line in *The Promise* is built around the psychological illness of Michael Gordon and the skillful treatment of the troubled young man by Danny the Freudian-trained clinician who plumbs down to the unconscious mind of his patient in order to bring up and expose to daylight the main cause of his illness.

For Danny and the author, Freudian psychoanalytic treatment is a road to liberation from guilt and pain. As a mid-twentieth century intellectual Potok assumes that a mental illness is entirely psychological in its dimensions. When dealing with another patient named Jonathan, Daniel says he must get him to "decathect for Michael" and break the "aggression-fear-hostility cycle" (249). Danny (and Potok as novelist) is a teacher/ disciple who likes to explain Freud to friends and students (269). (See Chapter 3, Psychoanalytic Theory.)

The dream passages in *The Promise* are also significant. In 1900 Freud published *The Interpretation of Dreams*. He and his disciples say that our dreams are the road to our unconscious. Also, we disguise the desires that are repressed by our superego and the anxieties that are too fearsome or painful for our conscious minds. Then we play them out in our dreams.

Dreams play a prominent part in *The Promise*, which in Freudian terms is Potok's dream. Michael informs us that he has many dreams (82). In one he dreams of sailing into the heavens with his new friend Reuven (82). Clearly he wishes to escape the painful world in which he lives and go with his "dream friend" among the stars he knows so well, stars that are friendly and constant. . . . He says: "It was a good dream" (82). But of course it is only a dream. He is earthbound in the real world still. Reuven also dreams of sailing again with Michael. In his dream Michael is trying to communicate with him, but Reuven can't hear him. With healing the dreams depart, for life becomes better lived on the level of the consciousness.

5

My Name Is Asher Lev
(1972)

My Name Is Asher Lev is the story of the difficult childhood and early manhood of an artist who was so different that his family and society tried to curtail the freedom that is necessary to an artistic soul. And it is a story of youth overcoming great impediments placed there by a well-meaning but uncomprehending older generation. The hero's struggle with his community, his parents, and himself is played out against the conflict between an ultra-orthodox way of life that sees no value in the fine arts and the secular world that values art for its own sake. The novel implies that it takes much strength and perseverance to be a true artist and that to be an artist is a worthwhile goal in itself. It also implies that art may be both an almost uncontrollable obsession and an unconscious rebellion against the power of parents and tribe. Thus the hero says from time to time, almost as if he were speaking to himself in assurance: "My name is Asher Lev." It is enough.

Chaim Potok is a painter as well as a writer. For ultra-Orthodox Jews paintings are often considered idolatrous, especially when they portray living things. So when Potok grew up in an Orthodox Jewish family submerged in an Orthodox Jewish community that considers painting pictures a preoccupation of the Gentile world (a painter is someone who comes in to do the walls), he experienced some of the usual discouragement of the artist. The stricter ultra-Orthodox society looks upon art as either sacrilegious, frivolous, or politically disruptive, and the artist as a dangerous outsider who should be shunned. No significant Jewish artist in the West—including Amedeo Modigliani, Marc Chagall, Jacob Epstein, Jacques Lipchitz, and Mark Rothko—has been a religious Jew (Kouvar, 291).

The painting that finally destroys Asher Lev's relationship with his family and religious community is one on the Crucifixion theme: *Brooklyn Crucifixion*. Asher's goal in telling his story is to offer "justification for his masterpiece" (Pinsker, 42). Potok created a painting with that same title while composing the final chapters of *My Name Is Asher Lev*. Writing in the *New York Times Book Review*, Guy Davenport said: "One feels that his subject was inevitable and that he is writing with deepest and total understanding" (5). In 1972 reviewing *My Name Is Asher Lev* in the *Saturday Review*, R. J. Milch said that "Potok's new novel is far superior to his other books" (65).

PLOT DEVELOPMENT

My Name Is Asher Lev is divided into three books. Most of the novel is set in New York City, where the narrator, Asher Lev, was born in 1943. The part of the city that is the primary setting is the Crown Heights section of Brooklyn where members of a fictitious Hasidic sect called the Ladovers reside. Asher's parents are Ladovers. Potok has based the community on the Lubavitch movement, also called the Chabad movement, a Hasidic community more liberal than most other such communities in that it has proselytized widely among other Jews in the United States and elsewhere in the world. It has been more willing than others to accept the twentieth century and even the twenty-first century.

Other locales for the novel include Manhattan, Cape Cod, Paris, and Florence, Italy, where the young artist achieves his greatness. Because of its subject the novel is an homage to Potok's favorite work—James Joyce's *Portrait of the Artist as a Young Man*. Both novels are in a category of works about the artist's life named from the German: *kunstlerroman* (story of an artist).

My Name Is Asher Lev is written from the viewpoint of a mature observant Jewish artist. He defends himself from the attacks of ultra-Orthodox Jews who have accused him of apostasy and sacrilege because of his outrageous painting employing a taboo subject: *Brooklyn Crucifixion*. The narrator looks back on his life from the earliest childhood memories to the time he is telling his story. The book is an apologia, a defense and a justification for his actions and his life. He began to draw in 1947 at the age of four. His twenty-three-year-old mother, Rivkeh, was one of his first models, and she would loom large in his life and become the central figure in the notorious crucifixion paintings of his maturity. As an only child Asher has a strong Oedipal fixation on his mother. His father, Aryeh, a brave and dedicated rescuer of Jewish survivors of the Holocaust, is often away from home, working for the Ladover movement. Asher's talent is immediately apparent and his mother indulges it although his father does not approve, for Asher is violating the second commandment: "Thou shalt not make unto thee a graven image." Thus the tensions of the novel are put into play: religious proscription against a compulsive talent; the individual against society; father against son; and Asher the devout yeshiva-taught Jewish youth who wants desperately to please his God, his rebbe, and most of all his good parents against the sometimes demonic need to draw and paint.

Asher is confused and depressed. His life becomes divided. He is tormented by bad dreams in which his saintly grandfather accuses him of wasting his time and castigates him for deviating from his duty to the Ladovers and the Jewish people. But Asher carries on with his art.

The leader of the Ladover sect, known in the book only as the Rebbe, is very wise and surprisingly worldly. When Asher is a teenager, the Rebbe realizes how powerful the creative drive is in Asher and how great a gift from God is the boy's talent. The Rebbe wishes that Asher could have followed the lead of his father and grandfather and become a major emissary for the movement, but he realizes that the youth will never serve the Ladovers. Therefore, when Asher is thirteen, the age of bar mitzvah, when a Jewish boy becomes a responsible man in the eyes of God and the community, the Rebbe introduces Asher to a friendly, secular Jewish artist of distinction, Jacob Kahn: according to Potok, Kahn is based on Jacques Lipchitz (Walden, 105). Kahn becomes a surrogate father, and he turns Asher into an outstanding painter as well as someone learned in the history and traditions of Western art. At the same time Asher becomes more secularized. Reluctantly he paints nudes because that is what artists do, and eventually he discards his Hasidic garb and cuts his sidelocks.

Asher's parents have been distracted by their own lives. His mother is profoundly depressed over the loss of her brother in an accident and her need to have a life of her own beyond that of a housewife. The sympathetic Hasids allow her to begin college in her twenties as it appears she will have no more children. A brilliant student, she goes as far as obtaining a Ph.D. in Russian history and culture and thus is able to help her husband in Europe. Asher's father continually sojourns in Europe, running an underground railway rescuing Jewish refugees from the tyranny of Stalin and the prison that was the Soviet Union.

Soon both parents spend most of their time in Europe helping refugees, and Asher lives in Brooklyn with relatives. Ironically, he refuses to join his parents in Europe but later will go there himself to study and refine his talent. Jacob Kahn becomes Asher's father surrogate, and art becomes his foster religion. Asher comes to love his foster father as much or more than he loves his biological one. His psychological and emotional need and his longing for his absent father create an unconscious anger. His embracing of forbidden art is the deep unconscious revenge of a frustrated child. Jacob Kahn, Aryeh Lev's antagonist, is a satisfactory replacement until Asher's ego is strong and he no longer has the need to search for a father.

Finally, in 1961 Lev reluctantly flies to Europe to meet his parents in Vienna, but he becomes ill on the plane. He is deathly sick in Vienna. His angry father suspects it is psychosomatic. His parents quarrel, and he is sent home. At age eighteen Lev graduates from his yeshiva high school and enrolls in Brooklyn College where he majors in sociology— "a safe subject [that] would not interfere with my painting" (295). Shortly after he has his first New York gallery show. It is a minor success. Another show the next year is even more successful. His parents return home and the family is reunited, but they have been apart too long to have much in common. The parents try to arrange a marriage for their eligible son as is customary, but Lev refuses. He is not ready for marriage and a large family.

At Kahn's insistence Lev goes to Florence. He must see and study the works of the great Renaissance masters. From Florence he goes to Paris and visits the house in which Picasso painted. Then he begins a long sojourn in that great art center. Everywhere he goes, he finds Jewish people who admire his father. He meets a comely Jewish girl the reader suspects will later become his wife, and after years of studying the great works of Western art, Lev paints his masterpiece, *Brooklyn Crucifixion*. It depicts his mother as a crucified person in agony looking out of the apartment window for her husband and son to return. She is suffering because the two men in her life are at odds. Lev considers the use of a crucifixion scene as merely locating a motif for great suffering not available in the Jewish tradition. Potok has said that for him as a painter the crucifixion has no religious significance but is merely an aesthetic vessel (Forbes, 16).

Asher's New York gallery owner comes to see his work and is stunned by the power of *Brooklyn Crucifixion* and another crucifixion painting. She tells him it is time for him to return. He flies home to New York City. When the paintings are to be exhibited in a New York City gallery, Lev tries to divert his parents from seeing them. They are happy that there will be no nudes in the show to prevent their attending and are unaware that their son has painted his mother into a crucifixion—for them a blasphemous betrayal of Judaism, since the crucifixion of Jesus long has been an excuse by Christians for the murder of Jews. It is for many Jewish people a symbol of the most violent anti-Semitism.

In the end *My Name Is Asher Lev* comes close to tragedy. Although he has triumphed as an artist, Lev is heartbroken at the reception of his crucifixion paintings by his family and the Ladovers and is returning to Europe, an exile from his parents, his community, his city, and his country. He has hurt the people he loves most. The saddened and disappointed Rebbe has said: "You have crossed a boundary. I cannot help you" (371). Lev is tormented that his right hand, the hand that paints, has served both creation and destruction. As he leaves Brooklyn in the snow, his mother says: "Have a safe journey, my Asher" (373). She is more worried about his life than his trip. The journey is the subject of the sequel *The Gift of Asher Lev*. Like Joyce's autobiographical hero in *Portrait of the Artist as a Young Man*, Asher Lev sees self-imposed exile as a necessary condition for a serious artist. S. Lillian Kremer in *Dictionary of Literary Biography* notes: "Potok, like Joyce, treats the artist's isolation and alienation from the family, school, and religious community, culminating in exile, as a progressive step that will lead to reconciliation of the artist's spiritual and aesthetic natures" (206).

HISTORICAL BACKGROUND

My Name Is Asher Lev covers much of the same chronological period as *The Promise*. The novel opens in 1947 when Asher is four years old, and it proceeds until Asher is well into his twenties. The Cold War between the Western world and the Soviet bloc is underway. The most important historical events in the novel are the frequent persecutions of Jews in Stalin's Soviet Union. Aryeh Lev and the Ladovers are dedicated to the rescue of as many Russian Jews as possible. They are trying to prevent a Russian Holocaust. The climax to Aryeh's mission is the death of Stalin in 1953, but his work for the Ladovers continues as he helps establish Ladover communities and schools in Europe and America.

In the United States the antidemocratic McCarthy period emerges and the Korean War is fought, but these events have little effect on either the self-interested Hasidic community or the self-interested artistic community. In *The Promise* Potok refers to the notorious Rosenberg case, in which Julius and Ethel Rosenberg are convicted of giving nuclear secrets to the Soviet Union and executed in 1953. Rav Kalman is amazed that their conviction has not led to a pogrom, and the American-born Reuven points out the difference between minority life in America and minority life in pre-World War II Eastern Europe (303). Unlike Reuven, Asher, also American born, shows no such awareness of the privilege of his birth.

In *My Name Is Asher Lev* the Ladovers and to a lesser extent the artists, Gentile and Jew, have little awareness or appreciation of the liberty that allows the former to live their exclusive lives and carry on their courageous rescue missions and the latter to take artistic freedom for granted. At the age of eighteen Asher would have been required to register for Selective Service, otherwise known as the "draft." There is no mention of this in the book. Did he dare claim a religious exemption?

CHARACTER DEVELOPMENT

Once more Chaim Potok limits the number of major characters in a novel. This device means that he is able to focus with a dramatic intensity on his characters so that the reader understands in depth the complexities and motivations of Potok's people. The major characters of *My Name Is Asher Lev* are Asher, his mother Rivkeh, his father Aryeh, Jacob Kahn, and the Godlike Rebbe. They are all good, well-meaning human beings even when they are in conflict with each other. "It is one of Potok's greatest achievements to have shown it possible to create effective novels in which good versus good is the central element (Abramson, 81).

Asher Lev is a young, brilliant, talented person who, in the tradition of great artists who had to overcome much to achieve fame, fights with a blind determinism to get what he wants: an art education, mentoring, freedom to paint, materials, and recognition in the world of galleries and museums around the world. He would also like to stay within his Hasidic tradition and have a good, loving relationship with his parents, but if he must choose between his art and the extended family that includes his beloved parents and all the other Ladovers, he will and does choose his art. The emotional cost of his emancipation is guilt and, at least initially, self-doubt.

The young must rebel, and they must win. It is the way of the world. The generations succeed each other. If one of the young is lost either to life or family or community it is tragic. So rebellion must be allowed to a degree. Asher starts slowly, insisting on drawing despite his father's disapproval, neglecting his schoolwork, then refusing to go to Europe with his parents. Later he cuts off his Hasidic sidelocks and paints nudes. Finally, compulsively, he paints and exhibits a work that violates a great taboo of his society: a crucifixion in which he has placed his mother. His rebellion is then seemingly complete and irrevocable. It has led him to a state he does and does not want: freedom from the world of his father.

Asher Lev is a character who continually grows as an artist and expands his knowledge of the history and development of Western art. He also learns to suffer the pain of ostracism. Yet because of his talent and the instruction of Jacob Kahn he finds a new religion. It is Art. His temples are places like the Museum of Modern Art where he, like young Potok, could gaze in reverence on Picasso's masterpiece, *Guernica* (Kauvar, 303).

Asher's mother, Rivkeh, like Asher, but unlike other Potok women characters, develops. When we first meet her, she is a twenty-three-year-old Hasidic woman, born and raised in the Hasidic community of Crown Heights, Brooklyn. She is slightly built and delicate. She had gone through high school in the Ladover parochial system for girls and upon graduation she married. Asher's earliest memory of his mother is that she was like a "gentle big sister" (7). When Asher is still a child, Mrs. Lev is thrown into deep despair over the accidental death of her brother, whose voice she continues to hear and with whom she thinks she is communing. For several years she is mentally ill, but when the opportunity to become a student again comes, thanks to the Rebbe, she recovers and goes on to a brilliant college and university career.

Her second great sorrow in life is the growing, irreconcilable conflict between her husband and her son. She loves them both. They make great and conflicting demands on her. Living the traditional woman's role, she continually tries to effect reconciliations, but to little avail. That is the cause of her suffering. She is torn apart and "crucified" by male conflict and demands. Like most women in Potok's work, Rivkeh Lev's life is

circumscribed by her service to family members. Out of respect for Hasidic tradition she cuts her hair very short and covers it with a wig. Even
the earning of a Ph.D. is undertaken so that she can help her husband
in his work, although she shares Aryeh's concern for the Russian Jews.

Asher's father, Aryeh Lev, is a bright, well-educated man. He has a
bachelor of arts in political science from Brooklyn College and a master
of arts in political science from New York University. He works, as his
ancestors did, for the Ladover movement. But he is too preoccupied with
building the movement in the United States and Europe and trying to
help Jews escape Stalin's cruelty. Perhaps people blindly locked into a
mission, even a sacred one, do not make good parents. Their love and
understanding is more for their God and the world than for those with
whom they live. Thus Aryeh Lev is remote and preoccupied. He is not
there to help his son with his studies and to encourage him. He is an
ideologue. The mission and the message are everything.

Worst of all, Aryeh Lev has no aesthetic sensibility. For Asher the child
in his formative years, his father is a man who squeezes orange juice for
him at breakfast and is forever leaving the apartment with the *New York
Times* rolled up under his arm: exactly as Asher the man will paint him
in "Brooklyn Crucifixion." The Levs had only one child, unusual for a
Hasidic family, perhaps because for Mr. Lev children came after the business of growing the community.

But Aryeh Lev is a good person and someone who is of great use to
the world. Unfortunately, he thinks that Asher's paintings contain a
moral threat to the values of his ultra-Orthodox community that has
suffered so much and is now struggling to stay afloat on a secular sea
that threatens to submerge it with luxury, indifferent tolerance, and easy
exits from self-imposed confinement.

Jacob Kahn, an assimilated Jew, is perhaps, after Asher, the most interesting character in *My Name Is Asher Lev*. Kahn is a great sculptor and
abstract expressionist painter. He is old, wise, wealthy, and jaded. He
feels himself a rival of Picasso and hopes to live as long as the Spanish
master. It is Kahn who shows Asher that his religious education is an-
tithetical to his calling as an artist because it does not value the pure
aesthetic experience. Kahn and Asher's father symbolize the two poles
of conflict in his mind. Kahn stands for the secular, the aesthetic, and
the individual. Aryeh Lev represents the religious, the practical, and the
collective. Aryeh Lev knows what is good and what is evil in the world.
Jacob Kahn does not. What he knows is what is good and what is bad
in art. That is what he really cares about. Asher cannot go that far. Kahn

informs Asher that he cannot follow the Talmud's prescription that every Jew is responsible for all Jews and achieve his wish to be a great artist. Art for art's sake is his motto.

At the end of his life Jacob Kahn is egotistical and human enough to be jealous of his protégé who seems about to surpass him as an artist and celebrity. The father figure gives way to the child. To the dread of the father, the son succeeds and even exceeds. It is the senior's desire and dread.

The Rebbe is full of wisdom, sympathy, compassion, and feeling. He is a tzaddik. He wants somehow to keep Asher in the Ladover community. Ideally, he would like to see Asher's gift used for the community's good. But the Rebbe does not recognize a purely individual aesthetic need and thus, in respect to his community's goals, despite his best intentions, he has made a grievous mistake by indulging Asher. He comes to regret his action. Readers must wonder about Potok's very delicate treatment of Hasidic leaders when in their minds they can't help comparing the Rebbe's small-scale autocratic power with Stalin's nationwide control.

THEMATIC ISSUES

A major theme structuring *My Name Is Asher Lev* is an ancient one: the child's search for the father. His father's extended absences and his inability to understand him lead Asher to seek another father. The Rebbe understands the need and provides what seems an answer: a great Jewish artist as a role model and surrogate. Jacob Kahn can teach and mentor, and he may even come to love Asher, but he is too self-absorbed in his own work, his own desire for fame, his competition with Picasso, and his waning life to give Asher the intimacy that only a loving father in a home can provide. Thus Asher fails in his quest for a father (Ahrens, 43). His unconscious revenge may be the *Brooklyn Crucifixion*.

The second major theme of *My Name Is Asher Lev* is the conflict between Orthodox Jewish values and secular artistic drive. Asher Lev encapsulates the difficulties faced by many observant American Jews. They are torn between the values, rhythms, and demands of secular American life and their desire to adhere to the key tenets of their faith, including keeping the Ten Commandments, regular attendance at synagogue, and obeying Talmudic law as it informs daily life. For the ultra-Orthodox it is harder, especially when aspects of their occupations conflict with traditional values. Asher's case is more dramatic than most, although his solution is more radical than most. Compelled by his artistic drive, he employs a central image in Christian art, the Crucifixion, ostensibly because it has become a Western symbol of human suffering and because there is no equivalent for that degree of martyrdom available in Jewish tradition (Abramson, 79). But it can be argued that unconsciously he chose a subject that unquestionably would destroy his relationship with the Ladover community and alienate his father. The result is that he will continue to observe Jewish law, but he is free to do it outside of the context and control of ultra-Orthodoxy. Presumably, he will pray in Conservative synagogues.

STYLISTIC AND LITERARY DEVICES

My Name Is Asher Lev is narrated by Asher "with a fluent simplicity that belies its intellectual depth and the technical skill of its construction" (Milch, 65). Potok continues to employ an instructive, accessible style: plain not fancy. "He uses no . . . ostentation of style. . . . One feels that his subject was inevitable and that he is writing with deepest and total understanding" (Davenport, 18).

Potok's ability to tell a story that is extremely interesting continues in this, his third published novel. The dialogue is challenging enough to keep the interest of readers looking for thematic profundity, while readers looking for a good read find themselves engrossed in a compelling tale. Psychologizing, so important in *The Promise*, has been cut back, and it is easier to follow chronology in *My Name Is Asher Lev*.

A MARXIST READING OF *MY NAME IS ASHER LEV*

What Is Marxist Criticism?

Karl Marx was a German-born nineteenth-century social philosopher whose major works are *The Communist Manifesto*, written with Friedrich Engels and published in 1848, and *Das Kapital*, published in three volumes from 1867 to 1894. Today's socialism and communism derive from Marxist theory. As Freud tried to explain the psychological roots of literature, Marx, earlier, had tried to explain the economic and social roots of literature. Marx locates the production of literary work in the economic and political fabric of the time in which it is written. Also he contemplates the political use of the work in the time in which it is read. As Freud tried to alleviate mental suffering, Marx worked for a more equitable distribution of opportunity and wealth to alleviate poverty. For Marx capitalists are reluctant to share the wealth that comes with inheritance and ownership, and so class struggle is inevitable until an economically just society is reached. That society will recognize that the true source of wealth is labor and that only laboring people and their families are entitled to the fruits of their labor.

Marx called the ideas of the ruling class of a society its ideology. It is used to justify the power of the ruling class. In capitalist democracies (as opposed to socialist democracies) the ruling class needs to convince the working class that the free market system that has made them rich is of benefit to all because all have equal opportunity to rise in wealth and power.

Marxist literary criticism has had a long history that can be divided into the old and the new, although both parts remain current in critical thought. The old highlights an historical reading of literature, placing the work in its social and economic background and showing how the work interacted with the political ideas of its time.

The new Marxist literary theory focuses on the use of ideology in literary work to either propagandize for the system or subvert it. The ideological significance and social significance of the literary work *is* its work. Since the dissemination if not the writing of the literary work is in the hands of the power structure, then the values of the dominant class are the ideology of most literary texts. Thus the work of the Marxist literary critic is very important because it exposes the most significant truths of the literary work: its historical context and its ideological mission.

The Reading

The overriding historical event in *My Name Is Asher Lev* is the same one that informs *The Chosen*: the Holocaust. Nazi Germany intended to eradicate the Jewish people from Europe and perhaps, given the opportunity, the world. In just a few years the Germans succeeded in killing six million Jews, two million of whom were children. The crime of the Holocaust is one of the greatest in recorded history. It is best described as genocide: the murder of one people by another because of religious or racial hatred. The ideology of the Nazis was and is fascism: a political philosophy of social organization that exalts a nation and a race above all others, that embraces militarism and conquest, that values women solely for their ability to bear children (preferably sons for the army), that raises to total authority a dictator, and that allows no opposition such as dissenting political parties or independent labor unions. Fascism is diametrically opposed to socialism, which exalts labor, strives for equality, requires a government to serve a people not exploit them, values women equally with men, and states as its credo: "From each according to his/her ability. To each according to her/his need."

The Ladover community exists in Brooklyn only because its members were able to escape German and Italian fascism and the Holocaust in World War II. Asher Lev is born during that war, but he grows up in the early days of the Cold War, the forty-five-year struggle between the Soviet Union and its satellites on one side, and the United States and its allies on the other, a worldwide economic and sometimes military struggle that ended with the implosion of the Soviet Union in 1991. Josef Stalin, the leader of the Soviet Union during much of the chronology of *My Name Is Asher Lev*, perverted Marxism into a corruption that included the desire for world conquest through communism, an ideology supposedly based on socialism but insisting on dictatorial leadership, a single political party suppressing all others, state ownership of all means of production, and the elimination of private property through forced collectivization. Stalin approached or exceeded Hitler in his blood lust. As a virulent anti-Semite he continued the work of the Holocaust in the Soviet Union but on a less comprehensive scale.

In service to the Ladover Rebbe, Aryeh Lev has dedicated his life to saving Jewish victims of Stalin's anti-Semitic purges. He has placed the collective good over his personal desires. It is commendable that he is willing to sacrifice his health, his well-being, and even the happiness of his wife and child for his brave mission. One could wish that his gifted son, Asher, had more feeling for the needs of his community and that his compulsion to create great art could have been turned toward the objective of showing the Ladover community in general in a good light. In other words, Asher is talented but ultimately selfish and so he brings shame to his people. He may not have caused economic harm, but he has caused spiritual harm. Asher realizes this as he sadly takes himself off to exile in Europe.

The Rebbe of the Ladovers is a wise and well-meaning man and he has tried to turn Asher's talent to use for the community, but his mistake was to introduce Asher to Jacob Kahn, whose doctrine of individualism and success at any cost, inculcated in Asher, perverts the good intentions of the Rebbe and turns Asher essentially into an art capitalist, striving for individual fame that will be accompanied by wealth. He has made it clear to Asher that "as an artist you are responsible to no one and to nothing" (219). Even after only one show, Asher is able to face down his father by noting that he has money to travel where he wants to and when he wants to (300).

The Hasidim have suffered very much as have so many other Jews. One can understand and sympathize with their desire to shut out a hateful world and give all of their devotion to God. But although it hurts no one, save possibly some of their young, the community does little for the good of the greater community, the people of the nation and the people of the world. They pay their taxes but do no more. They care very little about what does not concern their immediate welfare. It is their right to do so, of course, but a world of such communities would be one of isolated tribes making no advances toward a creative and healthy society. Instead the Hasidic sect appears to engender a self-righteous mind-set that seems to many people, Jews and Gentiles, to encourage a selfishness that is contrary to the general good.

The Ladovers, locked into the political and religious thought of the Middle Ages, elevate and exalt one man because of heredity. He has dictatorial powers to excommunicate and expel. He can say who will be educated and who will not. He can order disciples to take certain courses in school or pursue certain occupations and there is no appeal. The ultimate punishment for disobedience is shunning. The rigidity of hierarchy and ritual is stifling to creativity. Surely God gave Asher Lev his gift, and the artist must escape the community that would drown his talent in conformity. He does.

6

In the Beginning
(1975)

In the Beginning is the story of David Lurie, a sickly, sensitive, and brilliant Orthodox Jewish boy from the Bronx who grows up in the Great Depression of the 1930s and World War II, is devastated by his parents' loss of their Polish-Jewish relatives in the Holocaust, and after ordination as an Orthodox rabbi, decides on a controversial career as a secular historian of the Hebrew Bible. In the end, like David Saunders in *The Chosen* and *The Promise*, and Asher Lev in *My Name Is Asher Lev*, he rebels against his religious community. Yet Lurie's goal, like Potok's, is to build bridges between communities and to protect the Torah, which is, after all, the central dynamic of Judaism.

The title, *In the Beginning*, alludes to Genesis in the Hebrew Bible. The story, narrated by David, is his beginning. The entire first paragraph of the novel consists of one sentence: "All beginnings are hard" (3). David's beginning, filled with accidents, illness, and fear of persecution, is hard indeed.

Once more, *In the Beginning* is about Jewish education. Like Potok's earlier novels, it is filled with autobiographical elements. This time the setting is the Bronx, which is less exotic for Potok than the Crown Heights section of Brooklyn, the central locale of the earlier novels. The Bronx was Potok's borough of birth and maturation. Today the reader can still locate the Hasidic communities in Brooklyn, but Potok's Jewish

Bronx has disappeared in the tide of new immigrants and devastating urban neglect and decay.

Also, as described in *Wanderings*, Potok's father and mother emigrated from Poland after his father served in a Polish division of the Austrian Army fighting the Russians in World War I (Introduction, xiii). His non-Jewish Polish comrades treated him badly, and after the fighting was over and he had returned home, a pogrom broke out. In the novel David Lurie's parents emigrated from Poland after his father's service in World War I. Max Lurie has a jewelry store near the Grand Concourse in the Bronx. So did Potok's father. Chaim Potok and David Lurie have very much in common. The novel rings with authenticity. That is why the critic Enid Dame, writing in *Congress Monthly*, could say: "*In the Beginning* is Potok's richest book" (22).

PLOT DEVELOPMENT

David Lurie is the narrator of his own story in six long chapters. At the end of the novel we realize that he is speaking from a point in his life long after the events of the story. In the last four pages of the novel we learn that after David left home in 1946 for graduate school at the University of Chicago he earned a Ph.D. in Oriental studies. Then he married, published a book on Genesis, and visited the German concentration camp where his European relatives had been incinerated. Now he is telling his story as well as the story of anti-Semitism in the first half of the twentieth century.

David Lurie was born in 1923. As his mother is returning from the hospital a week after he is born, she slips on the front stoop of the apartment house in which the Luries live, and David's nose and left side of his face hit the edge of a stone step. The family doctor says that the infant is unhurt and the immigrant parents, awed by the seeming infallibility of a physician, believe him even though David develops into a sickly child tormented by fevers and infections caused by the deviated septum the doctor failed to diagnose. It would be six years before the family physician, Dr. Weidman, realizes his mistake, and many more years before David is old enough and well enough to have the dangerous operation that will repair the damage and give him a healthy adult life. As a result David spends an inordinately large amount of time in bed and is sensitized by his predicament. He is small and sickly. Often he is tormented by local anti-Semitic youths like Eddie Kulanski and his cousin who come close to killing David by attempting to push him into traffic. Eddie symbolizes all the brutal anti-Semites who have learned in their home and in their church to hate Jews irrationally to the point of killing them. In early adolescence David is unattractive to girls because his nose is bent to the side. That causes him another kind of pain.

In 1929, just before the Wall Street crash that led to the Great Depression which sucked the Lurie family down from middle-class life to temporary poverty, David happens to see a provocative photo in a family friend's home. It is one he is not supposed to see for it shows a group of Polish-Jewish men, including his father, the leader, with weapons in hand. They are a vigilante group illegally protecting their community from rampaging Russian Cossacks and murderous anti-Semitic Poles in 1919. Under Max Lurie they had turned the armed band into a society called the Am Kedoshim (The Holy People), a prosperous mutual aid society that together emigrated with their immediate families to New York City and continued to look out for each other. Later they worked to bring other friends and relatives to America. The great tragedy for Max Lurie, and for his wife Ruth, comes later. They are not able to convince their remaining relatives in Poland to emigrate to New York City before the Holocaust. In 1945, after the Allied armies liberate the concentration camps, they learn that not one of their many relatives survived the German genocide.

Meanwhile, as David grows up, he learns that he is named for his father's dead brother, a sensitive intellectual in Poland who, after marrying Ruth, was murdered in a Polish pogrom against Jews. Max then married Ruth, because he truly loved her and the Torah says that if a man marries and dies without children, then his brother should marry the widow and give the firstborn son the dead brother's name. The spirit of the dead David Lurie seems to invest the family as both father and mother loved him and think of him often. Young David sometimes feels that he is his dead uncle reincarnated.

News comes to the community of the massacre of Jews in Palestine in 1929. Arabs killed yeshiva students in an anti-Semitic riot in Hebron. The Am Kedoshim society is shocked, and it sends aid to the Jews in the Holy Land. Even there Jews are not safe from murder.

David is intrigued with his family's early history, his mother's life on a farm in Poland, and especially, his father's military career. Max Lurie had fought as a machine gunner in World War I for the Austrians against the Russians. He was born in the Austrian province of Galicia, which had been part of the nation of Poland dismembered in the eighteenth

century. Galicia became part of the revived nation of Poland after the
war ended in 1918. The Polish military leader, Marshal Joseph Pilsudski,
became dictator of the new Polish state which he led in a new war with
Russia from 1919 to 1921 (85). Max Lurie fought for Pilsudski as a cavalry
officer but soon realized that the Poles were so anti-Semitic that even as
an army officer he, as a Jew, was not respected.

In an incident when he was returning on a troop train from fighting
the Russians, he was attacked by anti-Semitic bandits who had held up
the train intent on robbing only the Jews on board. (One wonders how
bandits could hold up a troop train filled with armed soldiers.) Lurie
was slashed across his face with a knife, while his fellow soldiers refused
to help him (96). When pogroms followed the war, he and his friends
knew that although they had taken up arms and fought Polish hooligans
intent on plundering and murdering Jews, safety and freedom for them
could only be found in America. Max and his friends understood that if
many people in America in the 1920s hated Jews, the government did
not. The United States is a democracy. The Bill of Rights is for all.

The frightened David sometimes dreams of his soldier father in action,
sometimes dreams he is his father killing anti-Semites, and sometimes
dreams he is fighting alongside his father. But David consciously realizes
that he is no warrior. He will fight anti-Semitism later with words and
by protecting the Torah.

After the Wall Street crash in October 1929, Max Lurie loses his real
estate business. The Great Depression destroys his self-confidence for a
while. Later, he learns to repair watches and goes into the jewelry business with Ruth. In the interim, the family, which also includes Alex, five
years younger than David, has to move to a poor neighborhood in the
Bronx. Also the Am Kedoshim goes bankrupt and is no longer able to
help relatives and friends to come to America.

In 1933 history's worst anti-Semite, Adolf Hitler, is elected by the
German people to be their leader. New terrors come to David as he and
his family begin to learn of German atrocities committed against Jews.
American Jews face growing anti-Semitism at home, much of it prom-
ulgated by a Catholic priest, Charles Edward Coughlin, whose words on
the radio and in his hate-filled newspaper, *Social Justice*, incite young
Gentiles to attack Jews on the streets of American cities. David sees the
hate newspaper in the hands of Gentiles everywhere, and he is frightened.

David Lurie is brilliant. He learns to read English before he goes to
school, where he is bored. Daydreaming is his major school activity until

wise teachers give him special, challenging work. He also learns to read the Hebrew Bible on his own. Later he teaches himself to read German, although his father thinks it is a hateful language and refuses to let David read German books in front of him.

In his early teens, David is still sickly. He is pale, gaunt, pimply, and he wears steel-rimmed eyeglasses. Also, his nose is still crooked. He knows he is physically unattractive (282). When his father is depressed, David becomes depressed too. He doesn't want to go home from his Hebrew tutor's house, because there the atmosphere is warm and friendly. But when Max Lurie is working again, he is able to struggle again for Jewish rescue, this time from Germany, and paradoxically, the family is happier. A new Jewish political group arises and Max Lurie joins them. Potok calls them Revisionists, but they are Zionists who will fight the British in order to bring Jewish refugees into Palestine. Max Lurie's position is atypical for Jews at that time. He wants to fight back.

In 1936, just before the outbreak of the Spanish Civil War, the prelude to World War II, David enters a yeshiva high school, and he is an outstanding student. In 1938 the British and the French sell out Czechoslovakia to Germany at Munich. Time is running out for European Jews. In September of 1939, the Germans invade Poland, World War II begins, and the Luries' family in Poland never writes again. "The Nazi darkness spread itself across Europe" (335). The next year David enrolls in a yeshiva college in the upper west side of Manhattan that sounds very much like Yeshiva University, which Potok attended. There he studies toward ordination as an Orthodox rabbi. To his surprise, the Bible is almost never taught there. The religious curriculum centers almost exclusively on the Talmud.

David's brother, Alex, is taking a different tack. He loves English literature and is secretly preparing to teach it when he can escape from the religiosity of his environment. When confronted by the idea that he may be appropriating a tradition that is not his, Alex replies, as many people have: "It's mine if I make it mine" (342).

As 1941 and 1942 pass Ruth Lurie grows more and more depressed. Her parents and siblings in Poland have not been heard from. Rumors leaking from Europe hint that the Germans are killing Jews everywhere. Meanwhile on 7 December 1941 the Japanese attack Pearl Harbor and within days the United States is at war with Japan, Germany, and Italy. Hitler could hardly wait to declare war on "mongrel" America. The Luries have moved to a middle-class neighborhood in the west Bronx, near to the family jewelry shop.

David, the seminarian, discovers Bible criticism written in English and German. He is fascinated that secular Jewish scholars and Gentile scholars are producing historical and scientific studies that shine new light on the Hebrew Bible, while the subject is ignored by the Orthodox, who are righteously convinced that the Bible came directly from God and cannot be corrected. Anyone who studies dating and authorship is performing sacrilege. David is warned by his lifelong friend, Saul, that he is treading on dangerous ground.

Meanwhile, Dr. Weidman has determined that the time has come to operate on David's deviated septum. It is a dangerous operation and David is afraid. The operation is a success, and the long suspense over David's health and appearance ends. Not only is he no longer sickly, but he gets to kiss a girl.

In June of 1944 as the Allied Expeditionary Force is fighting on the beaches of Normandy, David is graduated from college, winning most of the available scholastic awards. In September he begins rabbinical studies. A brilliant teacher, Rav Tuvya Sharfman, becomes his mentor in Talmudic studies. Other Jewish families begin to lose their sons, many of them dying in action during the Battle of the Bulge in 1944. Most Jewish American men of military age are serving in the armed forces (408). The death of President Franklin Roosevelt in April of 1945 sends a shock wave of grief through the Jewish community as well as the nation. The Jews thought of him as a friend.

The war in Europe ends on 8 May 1945 with the surrender of Germany after Hitler's suicide, and the Luries await news of 150 relatives in Europe. They are despondent over the first horrible photos released from the liberated concentration camps. When the news comes it is unbelievably grim. All the relatives are ashes in a concentration camp.

Now David falls from the cliff below his college as he tries to comprehend the dimensions and the meaning of his family's and the Jewish people's catastrophe. The school, similar from its description to the Jewish Theological Seminary of America where Potok was ordained, is above a busy highway that borders on the Hudson River. David survives and, symbolically, is reborn. His mentor, Rav Sharfman, now encourages him to take the risky step, for which many will not forgive him, and go out into the Gentile world to study and write on the Bible, using anthropology, archeology, and linguistics in search of truth. It is his calling to protect the Torah through secular scholarship. His father is angry, but in the end he is supportive of his determined son.

David then sets off on his lifelong journey into the Jewish past.

HISTORICAL BACKGROUND

Naturally, the mature scholar, Rabbi David Lurie, is well aware of the history of the early part of the twentieth century, but the reader is unaware that the story is being narrated by a mature man. The authenticity of characterization and setting in *In the Beginning* forces the reader to believe that a young person is indeed directly narrating the passing events and the concurrent history of his time.

David searches out the Lurie family history. His parents lived through the turmoil of World War I on the Eastern Front where Austria and Germany fought Russia largely on territory inhabited by Poles, Ukrainians, and Jews, none of whom had a country of their own. David's father Max Lurie fought for Austria against Russia in the years 1914 to 1918, and when the Republic of Poland was established in 1918 he fought for Poland against Russia. Returning home to Poland he saw anti-Semitism and even pogroms reoccurring and so he moved to New York with his wife.

In America the Luries were prosperous because the United States was prosperous. The Great Depression, 1929–1940, brought them down financially and depressed them psychologically, but like most Americans they found ways to survive, endure, and keep the family whole. The Depression ended because, with the outbreak of World War II in 1939, neutral America became the arsenal for the democracies fighting Nazi Germany, Fascist Italy, and Imperial Japan. The United States declared war on Japan immediately after the treacherous attack on Pearl Harbor, and Hitler then declared war on the United States.

For Ruth and Max Lurie the war really began with the German invasion of Poland in September 1939. From then on, they no longer heard from their parents, who, it turned out, were among the six million Jewish victims of the Holocaust, Hitler's war against the defenseless Jewish population of Europe. *In the Beginning* ends just after the Allied victory in Europe and Asia, and as the revelations of unimaginable German atrocities come to world attention. The Cold War between the West and the Soviet Empire is about to begin.

CHARACTER DEVELOPMENT

Writing in *Best Seller* of *In the Beginning*, H. J. Keimig states: "Potok's characters are strong and definite. . . . They are caught up in the impetus in Judaic culture for learning, the treasuring of age-old traditions, the respect of fellow Jews as a community of support and assistance, the love of family and the love of the Torah" (302).

David Lurie is a fascinating portrait of a tormented minority child trying to understand an alien world that seems to want to kill him. From childhood on he looks for consistency but finds only contradictions. The statue of the Virgin Mary in front of a Catholic church looks gentle and kind, but the parishioners inside are the people who hate Jews the most. The young bully Eddie Kulanski tries to kill him by pushing him into traffic, but Tony Savanola wants to play with him and be his friend. David's curiosity is what ultimately causes him to break with his father and enter the secular world, not only to defend the Torah, but also to come to understand Gentile America in which he and his future wife will build their life.

Like the young heroes in Potok's earlier novels, David is fully believable and very sympathetic. Very few people come to maturity without at some time in their adolescence feeling homely and outside. We are happy with his escape from dangerous sicknesses, ill fortune, and the confinement of a well-meaning but narrow Orthodoxy. We are pleased that, unlike the experience of Asher Lev, the escape occurs without a terminal break with his long-suffering parents.

Max Lurie is an angry Jewish man—scarred, frustrated, and suspicious of almost all Gentiles. He stands for "the irrational and highly emotional state that the horrors of European anti-Semitism have created" (Abramson, 87). He is a leader, physically strong and scrupulously honest. He also is a military man, proud to have been a soldier, even if the army and country he served betrayed him. Yet he learns that his strength and ability mean little if his fellow Jews are not as willing as he to be warriors and fight for their lives. Max Lurie is a prototype of the Jew who fought the British and the entire Arab world to create a safe haven in Israel for the pitiful survivors of the Holocaust.

Lurie is also an Orthodox Jew, loyal to God and his faith. This loyalty almost causes him to lose David, but his love for his son wins out over his belief that David is making a mistake in seeking a life of study and writing among the Gentiles. Max Lurie is one of the most powerful characters in Potok's novels.

Ruth Lurie is an educated Jewish woman who speaks and reads several languages. She is devoted to her manly husband Max, even though she sometimes thinks of the sensitive scholar David Lurie, her first husband. Ruth is a good mother. It was only bad luck that caused her to fall when bringing the newborn David home from the hospital. Understandably, she succumbs to a deep depression when she no longer hears from her parents in German-occupied Poland. When asked to help out in the jewelry store, a diversion from her sorrows, she proves to be a good business person. But her life all but comes to an end when she learns that her parents and all her other European relatives have been killed in a concentration camp. There are, after all, some things beyond bearing.

David's brother Alex symbolizes the decision many if not most children of Orthodox Jewish immigrants made in that he chooses to pay lip service to the religion and the closed society in which he is born, while planning to leave both behind after he achieves majority. Alex will pursue an academic life as a teacher of English literature. When asked by David why does he not want to teach Hebrew literature, he points out that secular Hebrew literature is only fifty years old and simply does not have the history, depth, and accomplishment of over one thousand years of English literature.

Alex, like so many second children, has been protected and nurtured by his older brother, and thus has fewer hang-ups. He is quite ready to go his own way without guilt.

David's loyal friend and cousin, Saul, who is older, represents the traditional path of a bright, studious Orthodox young man. He conforms to the template of his society. He does not question his teachers or their teachings. Unlike David he will avoid controversy. Unlike David he is attractive to girls. His life is easy to predict. He is ordained, and one may assume that he will marry, have children, and lead a comfortable life as the rabbi of an Orthodox congregation in a New York City suburb.

Rav Tuvya Sharfman is another of Potok's very learned Torah teachers. He is less emotional about his subject, and with a pre-war Ph.D. from a German university, he understands David's interest in German Bible scholarship. His major contribution to David's development is his support of David's belief that he can study Gentile and secular Jewish texts, live among the Gentiles, and still be a good Jew. That is one of Potok's ubiquitous messages.

THEMATIC ISSUES

In the Beginning, Chaim Potok's fourth novel, reflects his preoccupation with the theme of maturation. Again a bright young Jewish male from an Orthodox or ultra-Orthodox New York City Jewish family grows up and successfully rebels against the constraints of parents and community. He begins to succeed in the greater secular world at the cost of punishing guilt.

The seemingly inherent conflict between father and son continues as a major theme in *In the Beginning*. But Max and David do not clash until David decides to do what his Orthodox father abhors, study the Torah with Gentiles and apostate Jews. In Max's opinion this can only help anti-Semites attack Judaism on historical grounds by trying to prove that the Hebrew Bible is an accretion over centuries, an amalgamation of texts, changes, and scribal errors, rather than a direct gift from God. For David and Potok this is understandable but wrong. Potok, in regard to the aftermath of the Holocaust, has said that his coreligionists will either "vanish as a people, or [take] advantage of the secret opportunity concealed within the persistent but hidden trauma we are now experiencing . . . to reeducate ourselves, rebuild our core from the treasure of our past, fuse it with the best in secularism, and create a new philosophy, a new literature, a new world of Jewish art, [and] a new community." This will lead to Jewish emancipation, "a release from the authority of the father in order to become adults in our own right" (*Wanderings*, 398).

David Lurie's great psychological problem, the problem for all Jewish people of Potok's generation, is trying to understand or find meaning in the Holocaust. Potok may have had in mind Rabbi Isaac Luria, when he gave David's family the name Lurie. Rabbi Luria, a Kabbalist who lived in Northern Israel in the sixteenth century, struggled to find meaning through mysticism in the catastrophic expulsion of the Jews from Spain in 1492.

Survival continues as a theme in Potok's first novels, but it is not only the survival of the Jewish people in a world full of anti-Semitism that concerns Potok. He foregrounds the survival of individual young Jewish American males torn between the pressures of a community desperate to survive as an entity even if individual freedom is sacrificed, and the temptations of secular American life in which God may yet be worshiped directly. Potok has developed this theme to the point where he symbolizes it in *In the Beginning* by having David repeatedly survive accidents, from the fall his mother takes bringing him home from the maternity hospital to the fall he takes when, overwhelmed by the news of the Holocaust, he falls down a cliff by his college and nearly kills himself. But he, like all of Potok's heroes, endures and survives. Of course, as David says: "Being born a Jew is the biggest accident of all" (66).

STYLISTIC AND LITERARY DEVICES

Reviewing *In the Beginning* in *Commentary*, Daphne Merkin wrote: "Potok's strength, here as in his earlier books, is his storytelling skills. His panoramic plots feature something for everyone, and the narrative thread weaves in and out of locales and periods with enviable effortlessness" (75).

Potok's use of recurring symbols as a structural device in *In the Beginning* is particularly effective. The Am Kedoshim photo of armed Jews stands for the need of the Jewish people to be unified, mutually supportive, and ready to fight for their lives, not go to their deaths like sheep to slaughter as so many did in the Nazi era. Another recurring symbol is initiated when David's friendly older cousin Saul tells the child the frightening biblical story of Abraham smashing his father's idols. David is reminded of it several times in the novel, especially after Saul's father says: "Sometimes you have to smash" (19). This recurring image implies that David needs to be willing to fight idolatry. As a secular biblical historian he will use historical truth to preserve the Torah from anti-Semites and atheists who use historical evidence to destroy the holiness of the great book by attempting to prove that it is irrelevant to modern religions.

As a child David hears the medieval story of the Golem of Prague from his cousin Saul (78–79). In the story a great rabbi uses clay to build a giant creature that roves the town and destroys those Gentiles who are planning to kill Jews. The legend is referred to other times in the novel. Finally, when the distraught David, having learned the details of the Holocaust, has fallen down the cliff near his college, he reaches into the clay to try to create a Golem. Of course it is futile, and anyway it is too late. Nothing can save the gassed and burned six million Jews of Europe (432).

Eddie Kulanski keeps reappearing in David's life even when the family moves to a poorer neighborhood. Eddie symbolizes the fact that anti-Semitism cannot be evaded by changing neighborhoods. It has to be confronted head-on. Ironically, David assumes that during World War II, while he is draft deferred because he is a divinity student, Eddie is in the army fighting the Nazis, who share his hatred.

A NEW HISTORICIST READING OF *IN THE BEGINNING*

What Is New Historicism?

New Historicism is a recent arrival in the field of contemporary critical theory. Its ancestor was the use of historical background of context in literary criticism prior to the advent and dominance of New Criticism in the 1940s. Objective textual analysis was the main, nearly only, concern of New Criticism.

"Old" historicism emphasized the historical, political, and religious background of a literary work, largely at the expense of interpretation and aesthetic analysis. It foregrounded facts and historical ideas. New Historicism began to emerge in the early 1980s. Like its ancestor it has a limited interest in the text of a literary work. But instead of providing unending background, it foregrounds the use of literature and other cultural representations in a given moment in the history of a society and the function of the ensuing discourse about that use. In its conception the literary work is influenced by the historical, political, social, and economic forces working on it, and it becomes a part of historical forces when it is published. Any age is awash with histories. Any age is charged with conflicting histories.

Two critics have been very influential in the development of New Historicism. The French philosopher Michel Foucault depicted the way various regimes achieved and maintained power by employing dominant philosophical worldviews and political theory, often reinforced by literature.

By opening and filling huge margins around the literary text, the American Stephen Greenblatt, a leading literary theorist, has brought to New Historicism a focus on the social, political, and cultural transactions current at the time of production of the work. The margins are filled with discussion of the influence of cultural beliefs and practices on the work as well as the social transactions employed by the writer in order to achieve the work.

Finally, New Historicism recognizes the way literary and other representational works of art reinforce power in society. They encode social energy. They circulate powerful ideas. They are a most significant part of the age that produced them.

The Reading

In *In the Beginning* Potok is very much the historian. Early twentieth-century American and European history is a distinct subject of the novel, with the depiction of Jewish life in the Bronx from about 1920 to 1950. Especially, however, Potok is driven by the desire to relate the important story of early twentieth-century, first-generation Orthodox Jewish immigrants and their children. Of course, it is his story too.

Culture is destiny. Potok indicates that Orthodox Jewish culture, with its great emphasis on moral and ethical behavior, was both a blessing and a curse for the immigrants. The blessing was that it kept them together and mutually supportive, so that cohesion made up in part for lack of and then loss of numbers. The curse is that moral and ethical behavior has little currency in the brutal world of this genocidal century. A small minority has little power. The tidal waves of history easily sweep it aside or pull it under. Max Lurie is a strong, resourceful leader, and the Am Kedoshim have dedication and solidarity. But what can they do against the Russians or the Poles or the Germans, or even the economic forces that brought on the Great Depression? What or who can save the good and caring people of *In the Beginning*, these "People of the Book"? God? Connection to a nation of their coreligionists, Israel, with nuclear weapons? Becoming more of a part of the fabric of American society? *In the Beginning* asks the question. Of course it does not have, indeed cannot have, the answer.

7

The Book of Lights
(1981)

The title of the novel comes out of the Kabbalah, the medieval compendium of Jewish mysticism. Kabbalists believe that the universe was created by a light ray that poured into containers, some of which broke, thus causing evil to enter the world. Pieces of light are everywhere. When the spilled light is gathered up by humankind, people will become immortal. For kabbalists, the two-thousand-year dispersal of the Jews is to prepare the world for the Messiah who will come when the lights are recovered. Kabbalists naturally would be fascinated by light, for God said "Let there be light," just after creating the heaven and the earth. Before light the earth was "without form, and void" (Genesis). Like mysticism, light is incorporeal. But as particle and wave it has substance, motion, and power.

In *The Book of Lights* Potok is addressing the seemingly universal search for the spiritual. There must be more to life than what is found in the material world. Traditional religions may be too bland for many.

Yet there is a second light implied in the title and significant in the novel: the terrible sunlike flash of nuclear explosions. Perhaps it is part of the spilled evil that must be gathered up and sealed safely until the Messiah comes or comes again. But it must be said that Potok prevents the novel from sinking under the heavy weight of intellectual probing by adding "irreverent humor . . . to keep his message from slipping into a soulful or guilt-driven apologia" (Manuel, B4).

The hero of *The Book of Lights*, Gershon Loran, is a young man who has a vision on the roof of the Brooklyn apartment house in which he lives. It convinces him that he has come to know the nature of the universe. His life takes him through ordination as a rabbi, into the United States Army, and to Asia as he seeks confirmation of what he believes to be the message in the vision: God created the beautiful universe, and life is the essential property in it. His life is enriched by a friendship with a young fellow rabbi, Arthur Leiden, who is plagued by guilt over his family's involvement in the development of the atomic bomb. Also, Gershon's love for Karen Levin helps to structure a life that seems to exist half in the world of visions and half in the painful present.

PLOT DEVELOPMENT

In *The Book of Lights* for the first time Chaim Potok drops the first-person narration and replaces it with the third-person direct authorial voice. Potok divided the narrative into three parts. Potok readers are back in Brooklyn at the beginning but other locales include Korea and Israel. More than half the action takes place in the Far East.

The hero, Gershon Loran, is a quiet, reserved, and lonely Jewish male. He was born in 1929, the same year Potok was born. At the age of eight he was orphaned. On a visit to Palestine, his parents were killed in a crossfire between Arabs and Jews. They are buried in Jerusalem. He lives with his aunt and uncle whose only child, a son, was killed in combat in World War II. They are all religious Jews. Their apartment in a deteriorating section of Brooklyn is small. Gershon has a dingy room with a narrow bed. It is his domicile until he is twenty-one, and he comes back to it after the army. His aunt, a housewife, never recovered from the death of her only child. His uncle owns a rundown Hebrew bookstore. Gershon's life is bleak—especially after the death of his favorite cousin, the soldier. Gershon was fifteen when the twenty-one-year-old cousin died.

But one clear summer evening, when Gershon is sixteen, he has a vision on the roof of the apartment house. He sees a mongrel bitch give birth. He is amazed at the process and reaches out to touch a pup, but the mother objects. Instead Gershon reaches up and sweeps his hand across the sky. Miraculously, he feels "the velvet touch of starry heaven upon his fingers" (6). The next day he returns to the roof, and there is no sign of the animals. Gershon never forgot what he came to think of as a vision, and he believed that if and when it returned, his life would be changed in an extraordinary manner. Later in the novel we learn that the vision of life took place at the same time as the first atomic bomb exploded over Hiroshima.

After a Jewish parochial elementary and high school education, Gershon enters an Orthodox college where, although undistinguished as a student, he is ordained a rabbi. Not knowing what to do, he applies and is accepted at a non-Orthodox institution, the Riverside Hebrew Institute in upper Manhattan. It sounds again like a version of the Jewish Theological Society of America. It is June 1950 and the Korean War has just begun. At the institute he studies for ordination once more. This time it will be as a Conservative rabbi. He is accepted as a roommate by Arthur Leiden, who picked Gershon because he is quiet and not likely to talk about family. The friendship is an on-and-off one because of differing career patterns. Leiden has an undergraduate degree from Harvard where he studied physics. His background is affluent. His father, Charles Leiden, is one of the nuclear physicists who developed the atomic bomb. He calls Einstein Uncle Albert. President Truman is a friend of the family.

Leiden's older brother was killed in action in World War II, just as Loran has lost a beloved older cousin in the war. Leiden arranges for Loran to receive a newly endowed fellowship named after his dead brother so Loran can continue to study the Kabbalah after his second ordination. Leiden seems to have transferred his feelings for his brother to Loran.

Meanwhile Loran has met Karen Levin, a Columbia University Ph.D. philosophy student. They become lovers, and Loran wants to marry but she puts it off because she wants to finish her degree and have a career of her own. He must do military service as a chaplain first. Also, she does not relish the life of a clergyman's wife. After graduation, when he parts with Leiden, and after a year of study with the great scholar of the Kabbalah, Jakob Keter, Loran volunteers to be an army chaplain and is sent to Korea. There he is lonely, hungry for Karen, and barely able to get enough kosher food to survive on. He is, however, a very effective chaplain, who chooses to serve with the frontline troops. It is 1956 and the long Korean truce has been on since 1953, but the duty is grim and dangerous. For a while Loran is the only Jewish chaplain in Korea. Potok, who served in Korea as a chaplain, implies criticism of the many Jewish seminarians and rabbis who avoided ministering to young Jews in the military because army life was hard and uncomfortable.

Loran is broadened by his Asian experience. He realizes that although he has always thought of Jews as a people chosen by God to be "a light unto the nations," more than half the people of the world have never even heard of Judaism but have religious beliefs and ancient cultures that serve them well. Japan is a place full of beauty for Loran, and he recognizes that the natural beauty God gave the world may be experienced anywhere. But it is Japan that opens up an aesthetic response to natural beauty in Loran.

Arthur Leiden comes to Korea as a chaplain too. Like a pilgrim seeking atonement for the "sins" of his father, he is drawn to Japan by his desire to see and experience Hiroshima, the site of the result of his father's dreadful handiwork. Gershon takes the erratic Arthur in hand, when the latter neglects his duty as a chaplain in his obsession with the nuclear holocaust. On leave they tour Japan with a beautiful and kindhearted bar girl as guide. Of course Arthur must see Hiroshima. There at the monument to the victims, Arthur offers the ancient Jewish prayer for the dead, the Kaddish. Gershon joins in. That night Arthur, in tears, asks forgiveness from Toshie the bar girl. She holds him in her arms and comforts him like a mother.

The friends return to Korea. Arthur wants desperately to go back to Japan to see Kyoto, the beautiful ancient capital, again. His mother, an art historian, had helped to save it from being targeted for atomic destruction. He substitutes for another chaplain scheduled to make a trip to Japan, and is killed when the plane crashes. Gershon is crushed at the news and cannot pray.

Separated from the service, Loran returns to the States and visits Arthur's heartbroken parents. He sees Karen again, but cannot commit to going with her to her job at the University of Chicago. They may get together again, but it appears the relationship is over. She is sad and regretful. Finally, Loran returns to the roof where he had his first vision, and this time Arthur comes to him as he says the Kaddish for his friend. Arthur's spirit adds: "Amen"(368). Gershon then flies to Israel to see his Kabbalist mentor Jakob Keter and to wait in Jerusalem for light or understanding.

HISTORICAL BACKGROUND

The first historical event that affects Gershon Loran's life is the development of antagonism between the Arab and Jewish community in Palestine in the period just before the beginning of World War II. His parents are killed in a skirmish between Jews and Arabs in Jerusalem. But it is in the post-World War II era that the book is primarily set.

World War II came to an end suddenly during two weeks at the end of August 1945. The United States, upon the order of President Truman, dropped atomic bombs on the Japanese and they surrendered. The atom bomb was developed in the Manhattan Project by American scientists and scientists who were refugees from Nazi Germany. Albert Einstein began the process with a letter to President Roosevelt. The Manhattan Project was located in Los Alamos, New Mexico. The first bomb was tested at the Alamogordo, New Mexico, Bombing Range. It was called "Trinity."

In 1950 Communist North Korea invaded South Korea. The United Nations voted for armed resistance to the invasion, with the United States taking the lead role. Three years of combat led to a truce along the 38th Parallel that is still in effect.

In 1956 the Soviet Union invaded Hungary to restore the Communist government. Almost simultaneously, the Suez Crisis broke out. Egypt had nationalized the canal, and Britain, France, and Israel attacked Egypt. The Israelis were trying to stop the continual terrorist raids that had made life in their country very difficult. They won a brilliant tank victory in the Sinai Desert. Later, under international pressure, they withdrew. The British and French also withdrew from the Suez Canal, and Egypt maintained control of the canal.

In Korea today American troops along with South Korean troops still patrol the truce line and protect the South from one of the last aggressive communist states.

CHARACTER DEVELOPMENT

In *The Book of Lights* Potok once more juxtaposes "two young men who are friends, although they are from very different Jewish backgrounds" (Woodman, 17). Gershon is a Kabbalist for whom light symbolizes God's enlightenment of humankind. For Arthur Leiden light stands for the terrible death-dealing power his father and other scientists released on the world. As a child living in Los Alamos, he was permanently traumatized by seeing the flash of the Trinity explosion and the bodies of birds whose eyes had been burned out.

Leiden tried to become a physicist like his father, but he could not

follow through because he came to see American science as death dealing, not life enhancing. He is haunted by the mass deaths in Hiroshima
and Nagasaki. Thus reluctantly he embraces a spiritual life by becoming
a rabbi and by joining the Army Chaplain Corps. He makes his way to
his surrogate brother, Gershon. Leiden knows that he will be able to see
the city his father destroyed, Hiroshima, where he can ask forgiveness.
He will also be able to visit the city his mother saved, Kyoto, where he
can submerge in the peace and beauty of the place. But chance, the ran-
domness of life, brings about his death in a plane crash just after he has
made peace with himself over Hiroshima. Yet for Gershon, the mystic,
the spirit does not die, and Arthur's spirit joins with Gershon as the latter
prays on the Brooklyn rooftop where as a teenager he first saw a vision
and felt the fabric of God's universe against his hand.

Gershon Loran's last name is interesting. LORAN is a tool of navigation, developed in World War II and used by ships and planes just prior
to the development of satellite navigation. Potok would have learned
about LORAN in the army. The word is an acronym for Long Range
Navigation. A geographical position is determined with the help of two
or more radio signals from different shore stations. That position then is
plotted on special charts. Gershon is trying to find his place in the universe. The Talmud and the Kabbalah send out different signals from
different traditions. Where they come together is the point where Gershon may find peace. Significantly, *The Book of Lights* ends with Gershon
resting and waiting in a garden in Jerusalem.

As a boy Gershon is quiet and observant. He has an otherworldly
quality that makes him more interested in studies of the Kabbalah under
Jacob Keter than in studies of the Talmud under Nathan Malkuson. His
visions, the loss of his parents as a child, the sight of his neglected neighborhood in Brooklyn self-destructing, his experiences in Asia, and the
meaningless accidental death of his friend Arthur, confirm and bring out
the mystic in him. The world of his future, even if it does contain marriage to Karen, and even if he finds a career, will never be as real to him
as the spiritual world emanating from the Kabbalah.

Two women of very differing backgrounds are presented as rounded
characters. Karen Levin is an intelligent, well-educated Jewish girl from
an affluent middle-class religious background. She falls in love with Gershon, but because she is career-oriented, and because she senses the mystical quality of Gershon's soul, she initially rejects his proposal of
marriage. Besides he must still do military service, and he seems to have
no prospect in life but to be an overworked rabbi of a congregation,

requiring a full-time wife and mother to help him. But the love and desire endures for the couple throughout the narrative. In the end the distraught and weary Gershon can't join her in Chicago. He must find peace, and she must pursue her academic career. She regrets the lost opportunity to make a life with a good man, even if it meant following him as a service wife instead of completing her Ph.D. and accepting an academic appointment.

Toshie is the name of the sympathetic, beautiful Tokyo bar girl who falls in love with Gershon and agrees to be his and Arthur's guide for the pilgrimage to Hiroshima. She undertakes the task with some reluctance for she has lost relatives there. Not having been to Hiroshima before, she is unprepared for the devastating effect the place has upon her. But as the symbolic representation of Japanese women (at least as seen though the eyes of American servicemen), she is able to put aside her depression long enough to comfort Arthur. Toshie sometimes seems like a caricature—the good-hearted, scarlet woman—but in the Hiroshima episode she emerges as a real human being.

THEMATIC ISSUES

In *The Book of Lights* Potok presents the most political theme of his career as a novelist. He addresses the often-asked question: Are scientists individually responsible if their work is used for immoral purposes? Specifically, was the dropping of two atomic bombs on Japan, the murderous aggressor, in order to shorten World War II and save millions of American and Japanese lives, an immoral act considering that tens of thousands of Japanese civilians were killed in the attacks? Additionally, since many of the nuclear physicists were Jewish, do the Jewish people have a special need for expiation? Arthur Leiden, son of a leading atomic scientist, internalizes the guilt and is poisoned by it. Gershon Loran, the mystic sensor, symbolizes Jewish recognition of culpability in the terrible deaths of so many thousands of Asian people who, unlike the Germans, had not targeted them specifically. This recognition comes in a mystical way through Loran's growing sensitivity to light, both the light of the life-giving sun and the death light of the nuclear blast. Potok, a great moralist, indicts the scientist, Jewish and Gentile, but implies that Jewish scientists, part of a people who have suffered so much, must be more sensitive than others to human suffering. *The Book of Lights* is Potok's contribution to Jewish expiation.

Chaim Potok talks about Talmudic studies in the four novels that pre-
ceded *The Book of Lights*. Now he chooses to explain in detail the significance of Talmudic studies for Jewish life as maintained by Orthodox
rabbis, scholars, and laity. In this novel, Professor Nathan Malkuson, a
world-class Talmudic scholar, considers the study of the Talmud the
most important area for Jewish scholars, perhaps the only study that is
fully and consistently worthwhile. The Talmud "affected one's life, one's
daily behavior. A Jew molded his life according to Talmudic law"(19).
To clarify the Talmud, to give it new meaning in regard to contemporary
situations, is the greatest achievement possible in Jewish scholarship. A
brilliant reading and interpretation of a passage in the Talmud is an "art
form"(19). It is beautiful, aesthetic, like a great painting.

The Talmud represents the rational in Judaism. The opposing theme
in Judaism and in *The Book of Lights* is the emotional, represented by the
Kabbalah—mystical, medieval writings that some Jews regard as a com-
plementary literary tradition to the Talmud and others a contradictory
one. Some Jewish scholars rank the Kabbalah as superstition, as valid as
astrology, and are embarrassed by it. Professor Jakob Keter is the spokes-
person in the novel for the reading of and respect for the Kabbalah. For
him the Kabbalah is "the heart of Judaism, the soul, the core" (22).
Whereas the Talmud is about the actions of Jews, Kabbalah is about how
Jews feel, how they see the world.

The war between the rational Jew and the emotional Jew within Gershon Loran encapsulates a central theme in *The Book of Lights*. Neither
side wins. In the end Loran goes to the holy city of Jerusalem to wait
for inner peace, or the return of the first vision of his youth, or perhaps
the coming of the Messiah.

STYLISTIC AND LITERARY DEVICES

Chaim Potok's use of the third-person authorial voice is quite effective
in *The Book of Lights*. The choice relieves him of having always to portray
a scene through a character's direct experience. First-person narrative is
particularly problematic when the speaker is a child. In his article, "The
First Eighteen Years," Potok states, "As an omniscient narrator you can
do things with language . . . that a first-person narrator out of a Talmudic
academy ought not to do" (101). Also, Potok is able to set more scenes
and show simultaneous events that occur in different places.

Pervasive light imagery provides a thematic structure for the novel.

Sun, fire, and the Firemen's Monument on Riverside Drive, the nuclear fireball and light burst are the major iterative images. At least sixty references to light shine on the novel's path. There are multiple references to the dropping of atomic bombs and the suffering of the victims. Light images begin off-handedly, as when Arthur and then Gershon grow sensitive to light. Later, the full horror of nuclear destruction becomes more apparent as the young rabbis approach Japan. Also, Potok amalgamates the names given to the two bombs dropped on Japan in August 1945. Little Boy and Fat Man become the Thin Man, on a window sign, and then the name painted on the side of a plane in which Arthur flies to Japan.

A READER-RESPONSE READING OF *THE BOOK OF LIGHTS*

What Is Reader-Response Criticism?

Reader-response criticism is a product of the 1970s. It is mind centered. It asks the questions: What happens in the reader's mind? Is every reading different from every other reading? Are some readings "correct" and others not, or are all readings "right"? The reader-response critic believes that the informed reader is the one most likely to understand the work. This school of criticism implies that the real existence of a work of literature is in the imagination of the reader. The text itself is only ink and paper. It becomes literature only through processing. Reading is a process. The American critic Stanley Fish insists that the reading of literature is about what a work does, not what a work is. The work affects the reader by leading him or her in the direction the author wishes.

The literary text, first existing in the writer's mind, is reconstituted, like instant coffee in hot water, in the reader's imagination. But the product is not the same as the original. It cannot be, because experiences, perceptions, and cultural backgrounds differ. In a sense, the page is full of gaps. The reader must fill them in with his or her knowledge, experience, and understanding. That mental activity binds the reader to the work and is the source of the aesthetic experience, the pleasure. So the reader actively cooperates with the writer to produce the work of literature. Communication through a text is like all others: two way.

Therefore, the reader-response critic investigates how a reader "reads" the work. The American critic Steven Mailloux, like Fish a Reception

Theorist, argues that the role of the critic is to show what the work is trying to get the reader to do, and also, how the reader responds to that demand. Other critics emphasize how different readers could read the same narrative differently. Indeed, the meanings construed from a novel could be different in accordance with the era in which it is read. Also, at any given time one reader might read the work as a satire, another as a moral tale, yet another as an adventure story.

The Reading

What does Chaim Potok want the reader of *The Book of Lights* to experience? Who are the implied readers? What does the author expect the informed reader to bring to the story? What effect does the book have on most readers? These are questions that can be addressed after the fact of the reading but which are felt or experienced in the process.

Potok is clearly trying to sensitize readers to the moral question as to whether or not the United States should have dropped atomic bombs on Japan. Potok presents both sides of the question: lives saved by the shortened war versus 150,000 civilians killed by two bombs. But he really is against the use of nuclear weapons, and he believes that the second bomb could have been dropped on a deserted island as a further demonstration of American power, thus sparing the lives of the victims in Nagasaki.

Potok knows that readers who experienced World War II directly may have a different perspective and opinion than younger readers and thus may read the book differently. A veteran whose life was spared because he did not have to invade a fanatical Japan may sympathize with Arthur and Gershon but believe in the necessity of the war-shortening acts. Others will believe America committed a great crime. And others, perhaps most, will come from the book sadly contemplating the difficulty of choice when the choice is between two evils. Which one is the lesser?

The Book of Lights asks the modern, enlightened reader to put scientific skepticism aside for a while and consider the possibility that mystical powers may affect an individual person. Gershon Loran sees visions and hears the spirit voice of his dead friend. These events influence his actions. Some readers will accept the vision and the voice as actually possible; others will believe that they are hallucinations. The reader, as with all works of fiction, must fill out the narrative with his or her version depending on education, cultural background, and experience.

8

Davita's Harp
(1985)

In *Davita's Harp*, another novel about the maturation of an artist, Chaim Potok strikes out in some new directions. For one, he presents his first heroine. Potok uses first-person narration in portraying Ilena Davita Chandal from age seven through fourteen. Second, he has her as the child of a mixed marriage, a nonobservant Jewish mother (thus according to Jewish law Davita is Jewish) and a nonobservant Christian father. Their religion is Communism. Davita samples the three religions and finds her fit in the religion her mother was brought up in.

The word Davita is a feminine form of David. The biblical David was a fine psalmist and harper. Davita's harp is a door harp, a passive musical instrument, like a wind chime, that makes a pleasant sound when a door is opened or closed. Davita, like King David, brings about a change in the Jewish people, albeit a tiny one. She and her mother battle against patriarchy in Orthodox Judaism and win a small victory in their congregation. That victory presages great change in Jewish worship. Yet Davita's struggle for equality as a female comes at a significant cost to her—so often the fate of pioneers.

Davita, like Potok's young heroes, is very intelligent. She needs that intelligence to survive in New York City in the 1930s, where militant Communism is hated by the general population, and where her Jewishness makes her vulnerable to the anti-Semites in school and on the streets. Instead of rebelling against the force of parental and community

Orthodoxy, because her parents are atheistic Communists, Davita has to find a spiritual path for herself. She samples Judaism from her environment in Brooklyn and Christianity from her saintly Aunt Sarah, a nurse and missionary. But Davita ultimately must find her spiritual life in her Jewishness, as her father, Michael, dies covering the Spanish Civil War as a journalist, and her mother Anne seeks solace in remarriage and a return to Orthodox Judaism, symbolized by her reviving her Polish childhood name: Channah.

Davita not only loses her father but also the man she calls Uncle Jakob Daw, a well-known writer, former lover of her mother, friend of her father, and surrogate father to her. Later, with a good stepfather and a bright stepbrother, Davita seems destined for some happiness until she runs up against a new kind of prejudice, not the anti-Semitism in her public school, but the male chauvinism in the Yeshiva she transfers to. There she, the top female scholar, cannot win the premier prize because it might make the boys in the school look bad.

Because Davita, a child, is the narrator, the locales of the book are limited to her various apartments and schools in Brooklyn and Manhattan; the summer resort at Sea Gate, near New York City's Coney Island; and to her paternal great-grandfather's farmhouse on Prince Edward Island, Canada. Reports and letters also illustrate locales in Spain such as Madrid, Barcelona, Bilbao, and Guernica as well as Paris and Marseilles in France.

Marcia R. Hoffman, in *Library Journal*, says that Potok "brings to life a story and a cast of characters which will not be quickly forgotten" (180). Edward A. Abramson, impressed with Potok's ability to work through the mind of a young girl, says: "Potok presents [her] emotional upheavals sympathetically and effectively" (136).

PLOT DEVELOPMENT

Davita's Harp is divided into three books. Davita, who was born in 1928, states that her mother was born in Poland. Her Jewish first name was Channah, but in America she called herself Anne. After World War I she left Poland, went to Vienna to study, and then, at about age nineteen, emigrated to New York City to work while living with an aunt. She became a recognized authority on the writings of Karl Marx.

Davita's father's family were Episcopalians from Maine. The Chandals came to America before the Revolution. Davita's parents met on the

Lower East Side of New York City and married. Michael was working as a radical journalist. Neither Anne's nor Michael Chandal's families attended their wedding. Their Communist friends made up for absent, disapproving relatives. After Davita, Anne gave birth to a second child, a son who died shortly after he was born.

The novel's suspense is sustained by several elements. The reader wonders what religion Davita will embrace, although with Chaim Potok as the author, that suspense element is minimal. More intriguing is whether Anne Chandal will come to realize that Communism as an ideology is as dangerous to humankind as Fascism. The reader also shares Davita's fears for the safety and even survival of her idealistic, risk-taking father.

The little family moves often because landlords and other tenants do not approve of the couple's loud meetings and radical politics. After the loss of her son, Anne becomes severely depressed, and Michael's unmarried sister, Aunt Sarah, a devout Christian medical missionary, comes to stay with the family and nurse Anne back to health. She also acquaints her niece with the compassionate and forbearing side of Christianity.

Davita soon learns that a radical writer, a friend of her mother in Vienna, is coming to stay with them for a while. Jakob Daw, a sickly, unkempt man, is like a jackdaw, a crowlike bird that is unattractive to humans but very intelligent. Daw writes parables about a bird who seeks out the world's goodness in music but finds too little of it. He stands for the freethinking radical artist, doomed in an era of almost worldwide totalitarianism. He was Anne's lover in Vienna when she was in her teens, and the reader wonders if she will take him as a lover again, but he is burned out. He loves her but without sexual passion.

In 1936, when Davita is eight years old, the Spanish Civil War breaks out, and American Socialists and Communists support the duly elected loyalist government of Spain against the Fascist Spanish army officers and their German and Italian allies. A few Americans go to Spain to fight for the Loyalists. Others, like Sarah Chandal, help the suffering Spanish people with food relief and medical service. But only the Soviet Union seems to be ready to oppose the Fascists with real force. Yet the world knows that the outcome of the war will show if the evil of Fascism will take over most of Europe in the next decade.

Because of her parents' vital interest in international politics, and because she is a passionate reader of newspapers as well as books, the brilliant child is very knowledgeable of, and much frightened by, world events. In her public school she is bullied and threatened by boys whose parents have indoctrinated them in anti-Semitism as well as anti-Communism.

In the summer of 1936 at the oceanside resort called Sea Gate, Davita meets her mother's cousin, the lawyer Ezra Dinn, a widower and a devout Jew. She also meets his son David. The Dinns will later become Davita's beloved stepfather and stepbrother. David Dinn becomes her good friend too. In Sea Gate Davita starts to take an interest in her Jewish heritage. Her mother does not encourage it. It is the singing coming from the local synagogue and the close family life of Jewish relatives and neighbors that warm Davita's heart.

In 1937, with Daw back in Europe, Michael is sent by his newspaper to cover the war in Spain. It is a dangerous assignment. Davita and her mother sorely miss the man they both love dearly. Michael is wounded in Madrid. Aunt Sarah brings her brother home and stays with the family while Michael's wounded hip heals. He will limp for the rest of his short life.

Davita begins to go to synagogue often. She loves the singing and the sound of the men praying. She can now read a little Hebrew. Davita learns from her father about a terrible episode in American labor history. Michael was in Centralia, Washington, on Armistice Day, 11 November 1919. He was eighteen and happy to be working on his father's cousin's farm before going to college. There he witnessed and was shocked by the lynching of a labor leader by fellow American war veterans. Michael explains to Davita that that was how he became radicalized. Americans could act like Fascists sometimes too. Potok took the incident from the novel *1919* by John Dos Passos (458–461), but it is a true story. The source is acknowledged in the novel (149).

Michael goes back to report the war in Spain even though he limps. Anne is sad and lonely. Davita has nightmares and prays to God for her father's safe return. Her mother now begins to sing Yiddish lullabies to her. On 26 April 1937 Spanish Rebel airplanes bomb and destroy the city of Guernica, and as Davita and Channah soon find out, Michael is killed trying to save a nun from the bombers. He was thirty-six years old. Nothing is left of his body. Trying to understand her father's activism and sacrifice, Davita searches out and reads Dos Passos's novel, even though she is only nine years old. She then does the boldest act of her life to date. She goes to the synagogue, and although women are not supposed to do so, she recites the Kaddish, the ancient prayer for the dead, for her father for the prescribed eleven months of mourning. Nothing can stop her. The other women, like Davita, separated from the men, begin to say "Amen."

Aunt Sarah is in Spain ministering to the wounded and ill. But Jakob Daw returns to the United States and moves in with Anne and Davita. Daw becomes a surrogate father to Davita, but, even though he is ill, he is soon deported because although he is an anti-Stalinist, he is suspect by the American immigration authorities.

Davita takes the loss of her surrogate father to heart. It is too much for her, and she tries to commit suicide by jumping out of a rowboat and into the lake at Prospect Park. Fortunately, she is rescued, but she has been injured and has had a psychological breakdown. Taken to her paternal grandparents' home and Aunt Sarah, she slowly recovers from the trauma and eventually is returned to her mother in Brooklyn. In the synagogue now, when Davita says the Kaddish all respond, men and women.

In her public school Davita is treated badly by the other students and even sexually molested. Transferred to a parochial yeshiva, she finds intellectual stimulation, and she is treated with respect because she is an outstanding student. In that school no one gropes her or calls her "a commie Jew shit" (255).

Anne takes more and more interest in Davita's fascination with Judaism. Religion now seems less a dangerous fraud or an illusion. Anne meets a Gentile college professor who wants to marry her and take her and Davita to live in Chicago. Davita rebels and refuses to leave Brooklyn, her yeshiva, and the synagogue. Mother and daughter fight and the decision is deferred.

In the spring of 1938 Davita sees Picasso's *Guernica* in an art gallery (Museum of Modern Art). She fantasizes that she is in the painting, running from the bombs, sharing her father's last moments of life. Years later, she writes a story about being at Guernica that greatly impresses her teacher. The reader now begins to comprehend that Davita will be a writer.

The next summer Stalin signs a nonaggression treaty with Hitler. Anne is stunned and broken by the duplicity of the Soviets. How could Communists sign a treaty with the Nazis who had bombed Guernica and who persecuted Jews? She is deeply depressed. She stops working and taking care of herself. The professor who has been courting her breaks off the relationship, and Davita will not have to live in Chicago. The Germans invade Poland in September 1939 and World War II has commenced.

Ezra Dinn begins to help Anne, at first as a relative and then as a possible suitor. He drives the ill and weak Anne to the old Chandal farmhouse where Aunt Sarah nurses her back to health as she did when Anne's baby son died. Davita stays with kindly neighbors in Brooklyn. After a few weeks Dinn brings Anne home. Her health and outlook have improved and she begins to practice the Judaism of her childhood, lighting the Sabbath candles and going to synagogue. Symbolically, she drops the name Anne and becomes Channah again.

Channah and Ezra marry and the two families are joined. Davita, now Ilena Davita Dinn, likes her stepfather and is glad her mother married him. The happy ending for Channah is the climax to her part of the plot. Davita now has a half brother, David, living in the next room, and although in time they both become sexually aroused by the proximity, their caring is non-sexual. In 1940 Jacob Daw dies of illness in France. Channah and Davita are deeply saddened over the loss of their writer friend, and Channah defies Orthodox law by reciting the Kaddish for Jakob even though he was not a relation. The next year, Davita's thirteenth, is the happiest for her. She has become a beautiful girl. Her mother holds Sunday study sessions for women, not to study Marx as before, but to study Talmud. In 1941 the Germans invade Russia, but the important events for Davita are her entering eighth grade and her mother's pregnancy.

In 1942 the United States has already become involved in the war, but Davita's war is with the yeshiva authorities who try to rein in her questioning mind. Potok now reintroduces young Reuven Malter from *The Chosen*. He and Davita are recognized as the two best students in the school and are competing for the most prestigious academic prize, the Akiva Award. Although she has the top grades, the school principal caves in to a powerful member of the school's board of directors who does not want the boys in the school embarrassed by a girl beating all of them out. Also, it would not be good for the school's reputation. The prize is offered to Reuven, but he and Mr. Malter refuse it. Reuven is gallant enough not to accept an award that another should have had.

The Akiva Prize episode is both a reversal and the main climax of the plot. Davita, and the reader, thought that there would be more justice in Judaism for women than in the Gentile world, but patriarchy ruled everywhere.

Davita, having crashed into a "glass ceiling" of her time, is crushed. She has little zest left for study, for where can it take her if there is no justice for a girl? But her father's and Jakob Daw's spirits come to comfort her. She will go to a public school where girls are not discriminated against if they are bright. When her sister Rachel is born, Davita tells the infant to enjoy her childhood because "They'll take it away from you soon enough" (371). The novel ends with Davita waiting for the time she can tell stories to Rachel about the door harp. Davita's painful experiences and losses have sensitized her. Her love of words and narratives has continued to grow. A creative writer is developing.

Davita's story is extremely moving. Adolescent women must identify fully with her travail. No reader can help but empathize profoundly with the struggles of the good, bright, sensitive young girl that Chaim Potok created in *Davita's Harp*.

HISTORICAL BACKGROUND

The historical background to *Davita's Harp* covers the period of the politically as well as economically turbulent 1930s and the events leading up to World War II. In the 1930s Fascism was on the rise in Europe. Italy and Germany chose Fascist dictators as heads of state: Benito Mussolini and Adolph Hitler. These nations became more and more despotic, racist, and aggressive, and more and more powerful as the democracies, facing domestic crisis because of the Great Depression, chose appeasement over confrontation.

At the same time international Communism as well as Communism in the Soviet Union grew more powerful. In the Soviet Union the dictator Josef Stalin made a travesty of the Socialist principles that had originally inspired the Bolshevik Revolution. The dictatorship of the people was in fact the dictatorship of a political party and vicious officials.

Because of the Depression, hundreds of thousands of Americans embraced Communism in the 1930s as the new wave of social order. They did so blindly, unquestioningly, while romanticizing what was really happening in the Soviet Union. One reason for the appeal of Communism then was that there was so much antilabor, anti-Black, and anti-Semitic activity in the United States. Another reason for the growth of the Communist Party in the United States in the 1930s was that only Communism seemed strong enough, and the Soviet Union determined enough, to prevent Hitler and the Nazis from world conquest. But in 1939 the Soviet Union betrayed world Communism by signing the non-aggression treaty with Nazi Germany. In the United States the power of the Communist Party was essentially broken because hundreds of thousands of American Communists recognized the hypocrisy and perfidy.

One major event in the 1930s, vital to understanding *Davita's Harp*, is the Spanish Civil War, the great prelude to, and rehearsal for, World War II. In 1936 the legitimate Socialist government of Spain was subjected to a military revolt by General Francisco Franco and much of the Spanish army. Franco, who became the dictator of Spain and ruled for thirty-six years, was supported by Nazi Germany and Fascist Italy. Only the Soviet Union aided Spain. In search of empire Italy had conquered helpless Ethiopia in 1935. Germany under Hitler was rearming to revenge the loss of World War I. German planes blitzed Spanish towns including Guernica, the subject of Pablo Picasso's most famous painting. Many freedom-loving individual people in the somnolent democracies volunteered to help the Loyalist Government in Spain fight Fascism. In America the Abraham Lincoln Brigade (really only a battalion) was formed, and it fought valiantly in Spain. The survivors were and are heroes to many Americans, but to others they seemed mere Communist sympathizers and even the dupes of Stalin.

In the end the Fascists won. Millions of people, mostly Spanish civilians, had been killed. The Soviet Union, whose support of the Loyalists was always lukewarm, signed with the Nazis, the Germans invaded Poland, and the world was plunged into the most terrible conflict in history.

CHARACTER DEVELOPMENT

Ilena Davita Chandal is Potok's finest female creation. She is an intelligent, inquisitive, individualistic child who suffers great loss as she is buffeted by history, patriarchy, and the folly of some of the older generation. But through her suffering, and through the intellectual's medium of serious reading, Davita learns how to survive. Practical Davita does not read to escape reality but to understand it (Woodman, 220). Furthermore, she is endowed with the imagination of a literary artist, and so the thought/talk connection protects her even as it probes reality. She intuitively knows the power of words and is always looking for definitions.

Potok is more explicit in describing Davita's sexual maturation than he is with any young person in his previous novels. We read of the stirring of sexual feelings, and we witness the trauma and the pride of the onset of menstruation. Potok's description of the young girl's sexual development is both sensitive and forthright.

Channah (Anne) Chandal is a complicated woman. Her life is a series of traumatic events. As a girl in Poland during World War I she was raped by Cossacks who also killed her sister and grandfather in a pogrom. As a result of the assault, and because she disliked her father, a Hasid who was always away from home visiting his Rebbe and leaving his family unprotected, she lost faith in God and became a Communist. She was well educated in Vienna and later at Brooklyn College. Anne truly believed that Communism would make a better world. Stalin's perfidy and her growing need for spirituality brought her to rejecting Communist ideology. She loved her husband Michael and is devastated by his death and by the death of Jakob Daw, her former lover.

Slowly, she recovers. She takes her childhood name again: Channah. She finds solace in a return to Orthodox Judaism, where, still a rebel, she wins a battle over the right as a woman to say Kaddish, the ancient Jewish prayer for the dead. Finally, she is happy in a Jewish marriage with Ezra Dinn, the liberal lawyer.

Michael Chandal, Davita's beloved father, is a righteous Gentile full of energy, a man who hates injustice. He is an investigative reporter for a radical newspaper. Michael, seen through Davita's eyes, is almost too lovable and good to be true. He goes to the war in Spain twice and risks his life to report the truth as well as to save a nun. But Davita cannot understand how her father could love a cause and risk—indeed lose— his life at the expense of his daughter and his wife.

Still Davita learns much from her father: to love and fight for justice, to seek truth, to reject materialism. He was born to wealth, a white Anglo-Saxon American male, the most privileged individual in the world, and he gave up this status to fight for political and economic justice and to marry the Jewish woman he loved and who was bearing their child.

Sarah Chandal, Davita's unmarried aunt, is a nurse and a Christian missionary. She is very devout, and she has dedicated her life to helping other people. In her good-natured way she tries to bring Davita to Christianity by telling her stories of Jesus and giving her children's religious books. But although Davita reads the books—despite her mother's disapproval—she would rather teach herself Hebrew.

Jakob Daw, a writer of parables, is like a fine-tuned musical instrument, "a harp of sorts," always aware of life's contradictions (77). He was a soldier in World War I and was badly hurt by poison gas. When, after hospitalization, he refused to go back to the front line he was placed in an insane asylum and physically tortured. His lungs had been permanently damaged. Katherine Anne Woodman suggests that Franz Kafka, the Central European expressionist writer, was Potok's model for Daw (235–236). Daw has Kafka's pessimism, despair, and world weariness. Kafka, like Daw, a Jew and a mystic, wrote symbolic novels of fear and entrapment, one of which is *The Castle* (1926). Davita and Jakob Daw build a castle on the sand at Sea Gate. Davita thinks it will protect her from the war in Europe. But her castle is America. Her father and Daw die in Europe; she and her mother survive in America.

Ezra Dinn is "an urbane and courteous gentleman." Unlike Michael Chandal and Jakob Daw, he is practical. As a lawyer, he tries to save Daw from deportation from the United States as a dangerous alien. He is religious but tolerant, and he has raised his motherless son, David, a bright Talmudist, to be a decent human being. Dinn is a good father to Davita and an understanding husband to her mother. He loves the Jewish community and serves it. Dinn may be Potok's ideal Jewish layman: the role model in Potok's first novel without major male characters who are rabbis or professors of religious studies.

THEMATIC ISSUES

A major theme of *Davita's Harp* is women and Judaism. With this novel Potok establishes full credentials as a feminist. Davita and her mother take on Orthodox Judaism from the inside as they challenge the separation of women from men in worship. Davita fights marginalization as a female in a fundamentalist religion. She had to confront anti-Semitism in her first school and neighborhood. Indeed, the hostile world of ideologues, racists, and warriors also threatens and frightens this little American girl of the 1930s.

Once again Potok uses a powerful opening scene to state a central theme of the novel. In *The Chosen* it is the softball game that foreshadows the religious conflicts in the story. In *The Promise* it is the tense gambling scene at the carnival that informs the nature of the gamble that is the life of a Jew. In *The Book of Lights* it is the rooftop vision that proceeds from the birth of the puppies and foreshadows the mysticism that grows in Gershon Loran. In *Davita's Harp* Potok creates the foundation for the two iterative symbols that structure the novel: a photograph entitled

Three White Stallions on Prince Edward Island, symbolizing the three adult men who love the child Davita, and a sweet-sounding door harp, made of wires and wooden balls, that announces comings and goings as doors open and close in the early life of a girl who will grow up to be an artist.

STYLISTIC AND LITERARY DEVICES

Potok makes excellent use of a symbolic door harp as structural device in *Davita's Harp*. There are more than twenty references to and images of the door harp in the novel. The sound of the door harp comes from the motion of a door being opened and closed. The instrument is played by the motion, not directly by human hand. An outdoor set of chimes is played by the unseen wind. It is like inspiration. "Inspired," by God or nature, a passive harp stands for the music, art, and literature that bring pleasure and make life bearable. But most of all, romantically, it stands for the receptive, creative, individual imagination.

The hanging door harp is like a mezuzah, a container with a scroll holding a passage from Deuteronomy that reminds people of the presence of God in a house. It is also good luck.

But the harp also sings sadly for all the intelligent and gifted women "who never had a chance to speak their few words to this century" (369). Lastly Davita's harp stands for the beautiful sound of a Jewish woman praying to God in His/Her house, the synagogue.

The door harp was originally a gift to Michael from his older brother who was badly wounded in France in World War I and who came home to die. The brother bought it in Europe and thought it might be magic, but it held no magic for him. He died young. It becomes Davita's after her father's death.

The other significant iterative image is the painting of the three horses running on a beach. It was Michael's grandfather's. The old man had farmed on Prince Edward Island in Canada. When he died the farm was Michael and Sarah's. The three horses represent the three men whom Davita loved and who loved her: her father, Jakob Daw, and Ezra Dinn. In one of the final scenes of the book Davita dreams of Michael and Jakob on two of the horses running into the distance. They are dead and the memory of them is receding.

Paul Cowan, writing about *Davita's Harp* in the *New York Times Book Review*, says: "Mr. Potok's prose style is so rich that . . . these pages have an enchanting quality" (12).

There is, however, one major stylistic failure in *Davita's Harp*. The first-person narrative of a child in her preteens who when she sees her mother naked comments on "the deep cleavage between the rounded buttocks" is simply not believable (258). Potok seemed to have given up on the first-person narrative with *The Book of Lights*. Reversion may have been a mistake.

A FEMINIST READING OF *DAVITA'S HARP*

What Is Feminist Criticism?

Modern feminist criticism came out of the women's movement in the late 1960s and early 1970s. A new feminist consciousness arose. It was influenced by the African American civil rights movement and by the impact on young women of Simone de Beauvoir's *The Second Sex* (1953), Mary Ellman's *Thinking About Women* (1968), Kate Millet's *Sexual Politics* (1970), and Germaine Greer's *The Female Eunuch* (1971). Feminist literary criticism employs several strategies: critiquing male-dominated society; writing the history of the oppression of women; differentiating the language of women; defining the issues of gender; studying sex and power; supporting equality and women's rights; circumscribing the distorted depiction of women in literature created through the male gaze; and rewriting the canons of literature, art, and music to include wrongly neglected work by women.

Feminist criticism has partnerships with Marxist criticism and psychoanalytic criticism, and even post-Structuralism, the investigation of how "meaning" is produced and an attack on philosophical structures built on the "illusion that language actually communicates truth." Obviously, feminist criticism is political. It presents strategies for opposing the ideology of patriarchy, the domination of the male. Women writers have been empowered by women to tell the woman's story. Women critics have been empowered by women to analyze the frequently negative or condescending portrayal of women in literature.

The goals of feminist criticism are to show what has been done with and to women in literature, to promote female values, to end subordination and victimization, and to encourage men and women authors to do justice to women. There must be no "Second Sex."

The Reading

Published in 1985 *Davita's Harp* is informed by the women's movement that had begun fifteen years before. One can argue that it is a feminist novel. The heroine, Ilena Davita, and her mother Channah (Anne) suffer because of the absence or loss of their fathers. They seek spiritual fulfillment in different ways, including Communism, Orthodox Judaism, and Christianity, and when they finally settle on Judaism, their birthright religion, they rebel against the Orthodox practice of separating men from women in prayer; prohibiting women from saying the Kaddish, the ancient prayer for the dead; and prescribing whom they may pray for. They are hurt by patriarchy, but in the end, led by Davita, they win a small victory against it: the women in their synagogue respond with their supposedly forbidden prayers. Davita's greater victories are yet to come for she will live to be a part of the woman's movement of the 1970s.

Potok is saying that his branch of Judaism, Conservatism, is the logical place for Jewish women because it allows equality between the sexes. Segregation by sex is not only wrong, it is entrapment. It causes great pain. It marginalizes half of a religion. And worst of all, it is an impediment to a woman's faith in God.

9

The Gift of Asher Lev
(1990)

In *The Gift of Asher Lev*, as in *The Promise*, Chaim Potok chose to write a sequel to an earlier novel in order to show the further development of a hero whose life he had already portrayed from childhood to maturity. Potok is very much an explorer of the human condition, and he is especially interested in the plight of an artist coming from a community that can neither accept the necessity of artistic freedom nor see the value of an artistic creation. Potok knows a great deal about art, and he knows even more about Hasidism. He delights in sharing with his readers his knowledge of a revered manifestation of Western culture and of a fundamentalist community endowed with and encumbered by a long spiritual history. Writing in the (London) *Times Literary Supplement* Brian Morton points out the advance in subtlety that *The Gift of Asher Lev* possesses in comparison to *My Name Is Asher Lev* (1182). Asher is a more complex character in his full maturity. The story is darker and more gripping.

My Name Is Asher Lev ended with Asher going off into exile in Paris after he was ostracized by his family and the Hasidic community for painting crucifixions. At the opening of the novel Asher, speaking at the age of forty-five in 1978, has been away from America for twenty years. He is still struggling to mediate between his ultra-Orthodox religious convictions and his need for artistic freedom of expression. But he must use his gift as an artist. That is the central conflict of the novel.

Asher Lev is a famous artist now. He is also a husband and the father of two children. His beloved uncle Yitzchok, with whom he lived for part of his childhood while his parents were in Europe, dies, and Asher brings his family to the funeral in Brooklyn.

Before leaving France, Lev tells the reader of the impact that the death of Picasso had on the art world in 1973. The king of art has passed on. He informs the reader that his own work had become stale, and that he had moved to the south of France with his family for a breather and to find new inspiration. From the time he left Brooklyn as a young exile, he has continued to practice his religion as a Ladover Hasid. Both Lev's art mentor, Jacob Kahn, and his manager, Anna Schaeffer, have died.

PLOT DEVELOPMENT

Again Potok employs first-person narration. It is more effective with the adult Asher speaking than it was with Davita as child and then as adolescent. After the expository information, Lev moves into the present tense. He takes his wife Devorah, their eleven-year-old, asthma-suffering daughter Rocheleh, and their five-year-old son Avrumel, to Brooklyn, ostensibly for the funeral and the mourning period. In fact he will stay for months and his family will not return to France with him.

Devorah, a writer of children's books, is five years older than Asher. As a Jewish child during World War II, she spent two years with a cousin's family in a sealed Paris apartment when her parents were sent to concentration camps and their deaths. Her ordeal was like Anne Frank's, but Devorah survived. She must sleep with light because of her long light deprivation and her bad dreams.

In Brooklyn Asher's mother and father are filled with joy that their only grandchildren are in their arms at last. The children quickly come to love their grandparents. The grandfather, Aryeh Lev, now seventy, is especially happy to see his grandson, and Avrumel takes to him immediately. Aryeh is less interested in Rocheleh because she is a girl, and girls are of lesser importance in the Ladover community.

At the funeral service, attended by thousands, the old Rebbe enters like a Mafia don, or a president, accompanied by brawny, suspicious bodyguards. He sits on a "throne-like" chair (20). The Rebbe's sermon contains a riddle stating that "three will save us" (20). That riddle is a continuing element of suspense in the novel. In the end it becomes clear that because Asher decides to leave Avrumel behind, Aryeh will succeed the childless Rebbe, and Avrumel will succeed his grandfather when the time comes. Thus the three who will save the Ladovers are Asher, Aryeh, and Avrumel.

Asher's deceased uncle Yitzchok Lev built a small jewelry business into a chain and made a fortune. He always admired young Asher's work and that interest led him secretly to collect paintings by famous modern artists like Matisse, Cézanne, and Chagall. Only his wife and his two sons knew about the passion Yitzchok had for great painting. The sons consider the paintings abominations. One of the sons, Yonkel, hates Asher as an idolater. It turns out that years before, Yonkel made an anonymous, threatening phone call to Asher saying that he was the Angel of Death calling. It frightened Asher into cutting short his one visit to his parents in his long years of exile. After learning that his father has left his valuable collection in the custody of Asher, Yonkel Lev is infuriated that he and his brother won't reap a fortune by selling the collection. He makes another threatening call to Asher. This time, however, Asher knows who is calling and is no longer afraid. He sketches his cousin as the Angel of Death and sends the sketch to him.

The suspense elements of the plot include: What will Asher do with his uncle's art collection? Will he return to France without the family he is attached to? Most important of all, will Asher "sacrifice" Avrumel to the Rebbe and the Ladovers as his gift or his payment for the pain his paintings have cost? In the end he gives the great gift of his son, and Avrumel is designated as the heir apparent to take over the Ladover leadership after a short reign by Aryeh Lev. One may assume that the fatigued painter will now be able to get over his dry period.

All suspense elements of the plot are brought to satisfactory closure without much surprise, except the matter of Uncle Yitzchok's paintings of which Asher is trustee. They remain in storage awaiting Asher's disposition. One thing is certain. He will not break up the collection by means of a public auction.

HISTORICAL BACKGROUND

Asher is a practitioner of modern art. Modernism—a style of art, literature, music, drama, architecture, and design—began for painting in the first two decades of the twentieth century with Picasso's creation of cubism. Picasso's death in 1973 is a dividing line between modernism and its successor postmodernism. As a modernist, Asher Lev combines cubism, painting employing intersecting geometric figures, and expressionism, paintings expressing inner feeling, semi-realistically or abstractly. He is not an abstract painter. He does not change his style with the coming of post-modernism.

Asher missed the turbulent sixties in the United States. France had its revolution of 1968, but Lev was an outsider there and not involved. The Ladovers prospered in the twenty-five or so years of Asher's exile. The character of the Hasidic sect changed. It grew materialistic as the members made money and moved from tenement apartments to large private houses with multiple major appliances and even swimming pools (41). The Ladovers grew more political and outward looking and now in the novel they try to influence elections in the United States as well as in Israel. They wish to have the most conservative candidates elected. They believe they are suffering and that they are in exile from Jerusalem (70), but they are not.

Sharing the widespread but not ubiquitous American prosperity of the 1960s through the 1980s, the Ladovers, like other Hasids, live in affluence, especially in comparison with African Americans and other minorities living in nearby parts of Brooklyn. As to exile, they could all move to Israel immediately under the Israeli Law of Return for all Jewish people, but they don't. The money is too magnetic, and remaining self-defined victims is the way a community like the Ladovers maintains cohesion. Asher's great threat to the Ladovers is that he has shown that one can keep the Commandments and find respect and success in the wider world. They don't want to hear that message. It is a siren's song to them.

CHARACTER DEVELOPMENT

Asher is a man in emotional turmoil. He is torn between his need to express his artistic gift and his guilt over offending the culture he was born in. That may explain what critics find so hard to understand: his continuing membership in the Ladover organization and his love of the Rebbe. He sees how the Ladovers have changed since his childhood. Though they indulge in the belief that they are poor, suffering victims, in fact, as he realizes, they have become comfortable, greedy, and materialistic. Asher notes their indifference to the suffering and persecution of others while they insist on proclaiming their own suffering and exile when Israel is open to them all.

Still Asher cannot break with the Ladovers because it would mean breaking with his parents and a culture that has connected him to God. Hasidism allows him to believe that there is a plan for the universe and a meaning to life. Asher has been blessed by the Rebbe, and in his heart he is bound to the old man as he is bound to his father and to God. Asher cannot live with the Brooklyn Ladovers or fully as one. He suffers for this. Self-exile is his atonement.

Asher is a painter version of the Jewish American novelist Philip Roth, whose novels, like *Portnoy's Complaint* (1969), are attacked by many Jews as examples of Jewish self-hatred. Because Asher has painted crucifixions and made "graven images," he is considered an apostate. Thus a great irony of *The Gift of Asher Lev* is that Asher's son is destined to lead the Ladovers.

Devorah was born in Paris in 1928 and is fifty years old at the time of the story. As noted above, her life before her marriage to Asher was a hard one. She loves her husband very much, and she tries to help him through his difficult period, but she finds so much solace in being a member of a Ladover family again that she would rather stay in Brooklyn than return to France with Asher. Also, she believes it would be better for the children to live in the more religious atmosphere of the Ladover community than in the south of France. The fact that she is a writer of children's books symbolizes her prioritizing her role of mother over her role as wife.

Aryeh Lev is seventy, but he is still dynamically engaged in growing the Ladover movement. Potok's portrayal of Asher's father has turned somewhat sinister in comparison to his portrayal in *My Name Is Asher Lev*. Aryeh Lev is as unsympathetic to his son's artistic nature as he was in the earlier novel. But now he appears Machiavellian in his attempt to influence Israeli elections. After all he is not a citizen of Israel. He is intolerant of gays and liberals. Many American Jews are liberal democrats, but ultra-Orthodox Jews participate in an odd alliance with Christian fundamentalists because of homophobia, support of parochial education, and pro-life sympathies. One aspect of Aryeh Lev's hard character goes a long way to redeem him: his deep affection for his grandson. Yet it must be remembered that the Rebbe has selected Avrumel as a successor, and Aryeh will be the next Rebbe while his grandson is growing up.

Asher's mother, Rivkeh Lev, is still the crucified woman waiting for her husband to return from his ambassadorial trips for the Ladovers. And she is still the mother of a son reviled as an apostate by much of her community. She continues to undertake the traditional women's role as mediator between husband and son. But she is also a widely published tenured professor of Soviet history at New York University. Her greatest wish, however, is to have her grandchildren with her for a long time. This wish is granted.

The Rebbe is an eighty-nine-year-old "Godfather" with a Mafia-like entourage. He has been intrepid in saving a great many Ladovers from the Holocaust. His photo is everywhere in stores and in people's homes, like a dictator's in a totalitarian state. He is kindly and clever. But his overriding interest is preparing for his succession. He is always controlling his flock. He has a worldwide network of informants.

In a sense Asher has two Rebbes, the Ladover Rebbe and Picasso, his secular Rebbe. They fight for Asher's soul and each gets a piece of it. In the end Asher seems able to paint once more, while the Ladover Rebbe has the bright male child he needs for the succession that will save the sect from disintegrating.

THEMATIC ISSUES

The great theme of *The Gift of Asher Lev* is the exile of the artist in the twentieth century. Lev is a disciple of Picasso, and Picasso's fictional competitor, the abstract painter and sculptor Jacob Kahn. Picasso was a Spaniard who lived most of his professional life in France. Kahn is an American who lives much of his professional life in France. The common experience of many artists, musicians, and writers in the modernist period is exile, sometimes voluntary, sometimes forced. W. H. Auden and Christopher Isherwood fled Britain to America at the outset of World War II. Thomas Mann left Hitler's Germany for the United States on principle. Marc Chagall, Bertolt Brecht, and Kurt Weill fled from Soviet and Nazi persecution for Paris and America in the 1930s and 1940s. James Joyce and Samuel Beckett departed Ireland for the European continent, searching for a more artistically fertile environment. Richard Wright and James Baldwin left racist America for Paris. But exile did not debilitate the modern artist and writer. It gave him or her perspective on the community and experiences left behind. To be an outsider—an exile, a refugee—is to be an acutely aware observer.

Near the end of *My Name Is Asher Lev* the artist created the two crucifixion paintings that make his international reputation and guarantee his exile from his native Brooklyn. He moved from the anti-aesthetic intolerance of the Hasidim to liberal, artist-loving Paris. Lev is in exile during most of *The Gift of Asher Lev*. But the call of one's childhood culture is strong. Asher is tempted to return permanently to the stifling Brooklyn Hasidic community filled with people who hate him and his work. He wants to meet the needs of his parents, the desire of his parentless wife to live in a caring Jewish community, and the wish of the beloved Rebbe to make Lev's son his successor.

But Lev can only paint in exile, in the light of the south of France, and he must ransom his art by giving the Rebbe his son. The gift of Asher Lev is like one of his paintings: "The Sacrifice of Isaac." The gift is Avrumel.

Asher's French home is in a village called Saint-Paul. Did Asher unconsciously choose Saint-Paul because the words symbolized his betrayal and exile? Did the words daily flagellate him?

The other major theme in *The Gift of Asher Lev* is the conflict between father and son. It continues from *My Name Is Asher Lev*. Asher and Aryeh are intelligent, educated men. They have affection for each other. They worship the same God in the same way. But Aryeh can never understand his son's compulsive need for artistic expression. He is convinced that Asher's dedication to art is a willful rebellion against what a psychoanalyst calls the Law of the Father, the superego power of the male parent. Thus Asher seems to affront God's surrogates: the Rebbe and Aryeh. As is traditional, women try to mediate. Rivkeh tried and suffered failure in *My Name Is Asher Lev*, and Devorah tries and fails in *The Gift of Asher Lev*. Only a truce, made possible by great distance and the sacrifice of Avrumel, prevents the destruction of the family. Because the family is a symbolic microcosm of the community, the sacrifice by, and the exile of, Asher the scapegoat preserves the community too.

STYLISTIC AND LITERARY DEVICES

Potok is very good with descriptions in *The Gift of Asher Lev*. Characters stand out, and the settings—especially the Hasidic world of Crown Heights, Brooklyn, and Asher's Paris of backstreets and small museums—are described as if Potok were painting them. Asher appears in "baggy trousers, rumpled shirt, windbreaker, and fisherman's cap. Weary, bearded, and somewhat bedraggled" (77). He is an artist without

personal vanity, making perhaps an unconscious counterculture statement with his dress. To have no vanity is to be free. And freedom is
Asher the artist's great need, second only to his faith.

An unusual structural device used by Potok in *The Gift of Asher Lev* is
the proliferation of images of, descriptions of, and simple references to
the Rebbe. It is as if he is omnipresent—like a spirit. As the novel uses
first-person narrative, it appears that the narrator, Asher, unconsciously
is struggling without success against being submerged in an ideology
that would chain the artist in him. The scores of references to the Rebbe
indicate that Asher fails to slip the chains until he gives the gift of his
son to the Rebbe to get back the gift of his artistic soul.

Writing in the (London) *Times Literary Supplement* Brian Morton praises
Potok's skillful use of flashbacks to remind readers of events in *My Name
Is Asher Lev* that must be known in order to understand the sequel (1182).
In fact a reader would really not have to read *My Name Is Asher Lev* to
understand and appreciate *The Gift of Asher Lev*.

Potok has little humor in his novels. *The Gift of Asher Lev* and *I Am the
Clay* have least of all. The author's view of the human condition dark-
ened as his work progressed.

A MARXIST READING OF *THE GIFT OF ASHER LEV*

Although as an artist Asher Lev sketches and paints the poor, the
needy, the victims of police brutality, and the victims of atomic bombing,
because his paintings make money for him and even more money for
his dealer, collectors, and investors, he has appropriated and used his
subjects. Furthermore, he has commercialized himself and inadvertently
employed his gift to support an exploitive system.

The Ladover community has deviated from full devotion to the Deity
to crass materialism and a struggle for worldly political power in the
United States and especially Israel. Its members employ workers, but
they themselves are not workers, they are grasping bourgeoisie. Their
homes are grand and fully equipped with all the modern conveniences.
The women are wigged expensively and wear high-fashion clothes. The
Ladovers harbor malice toward another Hasidic sect, "their sworn enemies" (91). Perversely, they do not employ nonobservant Jews as teachers
but do employ Christians. Other Jews may have subversive liberal ideas.
The Ladover community is intolerant of political liberals and gays. In
other words the Ladovers scrupulously obey the letter of the Law and

demolish the spirit of the Law. They have been corrupted by American capitalism and thus are emblematic of much that is wrong in our society. That a sensitive thinker like Asher remains committed to the Ladovers shows the power of a charismatic leader in a highly motivated religious sect.

10

I Am the Clay
(1992)

I Am the Clay is set in Korea during the 1950–1953 war. As in *The Book of Lights* Potok makes use of his experience as an army chaplain in Korea from 1955 to 1957. For the first time as a novelist Potok has set aside Jewish life in Brooklyn and the Bronx to write about suffering human beings who probably never heard of Judaism or the Holocaust. *I Am the Clay* is the story of what happens in war to ordinary people. In this case it is an old peasant couple fleeing invading armies who save a severely wounded orphan boy. The three struggle to survive as poor families have done from prehistoric times. Their enemies are not political but hunger, disease, cold, and man's inhumanity to man. Potok's depiction of a poor Asian couple's desperate attempt to stay alive is reminiscent of Pearl Buck's masterpiece of Chinese peasant life, *The Good Earth* (1931). In both books the central character, a peasant woman, encapsulates the enduring life force in humanity.

The peasant woman, who long ago lost her only child, is determined to save the boy. The old farmer is bent on his and his wife's survival. The boy is extra baggage to him, but the woman prevails, and the boy lives to participate in their epic journey through the hell that is a war-ravished country. Theologian Potok explores the spiritual life of these good people from the other side of the world.

Ever daring in his violation of Orthodox Jewish taboos, Potok took the title *I Am the Clay* from a Christian hymn. The peasant woman's mother learned the song from missionaries and taught it to her daughter. The old peasant woman does not know the meaning of the words: "Have thine own way Lord, have thine own way. Thou art the potter, I am the clay." She can also make the sign of the Cross, ignorant of its significance. Yet the woman acts out Christian virtues in her short life after becoming a refugee. In the spiritual world words and signs may have intrinsic power beyond their meaning.

But most significantly, Potok portrays in the novel a family's epic journey, one that is filled with danger and suffering. The journey ends in hope and safety for man and boy. But the woman, the nurturer and sustainer, wears out her life for those she loves. The old peasants and the boy have profound spiritual sides. They believe in the power of their deceased ancestors to aid them. The old woman, without realizing it, has called upon the One God of the universe with her song and her sign. Potok implies that the keys to survival in a world in chaos are spirituality and an instinctive bond with others. We badly need each other. Elemental life may be nasty, brutish, and short, but it is not without purpose and value. *I Am the Clay* is not a book the reader will soon forget.

PLOT DEVELOPMENT

The story begins as the South Korean and the United States armies retreated down the Korean peninsula a second time. The huge Chinese army has surprised the Allies near the Yalu River in North Korea and driven them and thousands of Korean refugees to Seoul in the south. An elderly peasant couple in a refugee column come upon an abandoned, badly wounded boy. The old man wants to leave the child, who seems to be dying. The wife insists on trying to save him. They place the boy in their hand-drawn wagon and pull their way through a landscape of death and destruction to Seoul, the ravished capital of South Korea. Along the way the woman risks her life stopping an ambulance until the driver gives her an antibiotic powder that ultimately saves the child's life. In Seoul they barter for rice and even eat a dog to survive.

The old woman remembers their only child, a son who died in infancy, and she will not give up on the orphan. Refused medical aid at an army hospital, she pulls shrapnel from the wound and sews it up. The old man finds a cache of scrap wood and that helps to keep them alive in the winter nights.

It is not until page 55, near the end of Book One, that the boy is well enough to reveal his name, Kim Sin Gyu, and that he is eleven years old and the sole survivor of his family. His father was a scholar and a poet. The Communists killed him along with the others. Moving south the little family takes refuge in a mountain cave where each successively falls ill with fever and is near death, but again they help each other to survive.

On the road once more they arrive at a refugee camp in sight of an American army compound where the soldiers are warm and well fed. But the refugees surrounding the camp are so cold and hungry that the young girls must prostitute themselves to the soldiers in order for their families to survive. Young boys roam in packs looking for things to steal. The soldiers allow dogs in their camp and feed them but keep the refugees out with armed guards.

Despite the ordeal the old woman continues to believe in the good spirits of the earth and sky. She also finds comfort in the words of the Christian hymn her mother taught her, words she does not understand; "Have thine own way Lord, have thine own way" (121). She makes the sign of the Cross in silence and as it gives her some peace it also seems to sanctify her in the mind of the reader.

Finally it is safe for the old couple to return to their village north of Seoul; the boy goes with them. The village has somehow been spared destruction, and a United States army medical compound is nearby. The reader is in suspense as to whether or not Kim will stay with his new family. After a short while Kim leaves to find the village of his birth. It has been devastated. No one knows him. So he returns to his new and now only family and goes to work for the Americans. The money he earns helps his new family eat well and even buy an ox to do the plowing so the old woman no longer has to pull the plow.

Then the old woman suffers a stroke as she is washing clothes in a stream. She slips into the water having just thought of the sounds of the Christian hymn she learned as a child: "Have thine own way Lord" (195). Unbeknownst to her, in a state of grace, she has undergone baptism. The other women pull her out and she dies that night.

At the end Potok connects *I Am the Clay* with *The Book of Lights*. The medical compound, the same one that is in the latter novel, is plagued by thieves. Kim Sin Gyu remains honest. He learns English quickly. When the base is relocated, the old woman's grave is disturbed. It must be moved to the other side of a hill. Kim and the old man dig up the old woman's body and make a new grave for her.

Kim serves a Jewish chaplain, "a troubled, dark-haired man in his mid-twenties" who might be Potok. The rabbi appreciates the boy's intelligence and integrity. He arranges for Kim to go to Seoul for education and the chance of a good life. Has a kind of miracle happened? Kim has been saved by the goodness, perhaps the holiness, of an old Korean woman who saves a child she does not even know.

HISTORICAL BACKGROUND

In 1950 Communist North Korea with Chinese support invaded South Korea. The United Nations voted for armed resistance to the invasion, with the United States taking the lead role. At first North Korean forces drove South Korean and United States forces out of Seoul, which was devastated. The Allies retreated until they maintained only a toehold at Pusan. Then the United Nations commander, General Douglas MacArthur, executed a brilliant amphibious maneuver and outflanked the North Korean army which was forced back to the Chinese border. Alarmed by Allied forces so close to their territory, the Chinese entered the war in full force and drove the Allies back down to the 38th Parallel where the conflict had started. Three years of combat led to a truce along the 38th Parallel that is still in effect. Unfortunately, parts of the Korean peninsula were overrun and ravished three times. Almost one million people died from the fighting, disease, and starvation.

While the background to *I Am the Clay* is one of the "hot" wars that studded the forty-three-year Cold War, the novel is not an anticommunist diatribe. Even with four armies battling in the Korean War—North Korean, South Korean, Chinese, and United Nations (mostly American)—it is often impossible in the book to determine which army at which moment is causing civilian suffering, although, historically speaking, the organized murder and terror of civilians was programmed by the North Korean and Chinese armies.

CHARACTER DEVELOPMENT

The old peasant woman is both a saintly figure and an archetypal mother figure, "diminutive, brown, wrinkled; kindness shining in dark eyes set in valleys webbed and serried like earth in drought" (43). She will do anything to save her "family"—her ungrateful husband and Kim the orphan to whom she has transferred her maternal love. Later her face is the "color of parched earth" (196). She is a part of nature, as basic as the clay under her feet. Potok has created a magnificent character. She symbolizes sacrificing motherhood and strong, courageous womanhood simultaneously. The life force drives her. She is a nurturer. Unlike her dour husband she lives in hope but remains always resigned to fate or the will of her gods and spirits. Yet the God of the universe has not ignored her. Without the old woman neither Kim nor the old man would have survived. She risks beatings or shooting in order to help the males in her stewardship. She saves Kim by begging medicine, removing the shrapnel from his body, sewing the wound, and biting out the stitches with her teeth. She would feed him with her breasts if she could. What would a mother not do to save her child? Her surrogate son will not die, nor will he ever forget her.

The old woman's death is not tragic. She has no regrets. She has served the living as she wanted to do. She goes to a much earned and needed rest. We all hope, as she believed, that there is a spiritual world holding a place for her. Potok has great respect and admiration for women.

Kim Sin Gyu is a suffering or dying child for much of the novel. As he begins to recover, thanks to the ministrations of the old woman, he develops into an intelligent, caring person ready to face life again even after experiencing the death of his parents, siblings, and extended family at the hands of the North Koreans and Chinese. Yet he bears no hatred. Rather he is infused with the love and kindness he has learned from his surrogate mother. Kim is a decent human being despite the savagery and corruption that is everywhere around him. He has maintained the virtues and the spirituality of his village upbringing. Alas, he is rather too good, too untainted, to be fully credible.

The old man is a self-centered peasant intent at surviving the turmoil into which he has been thrust. His wife has been a great disappointment because she has not produced a surviving child. He especially wanted a son to help him with the farming, succor him in his old age, and carry on the family name. His wife has washed, cooked, cleaned for him, and even pulled the plow when they had no ox. She nursed him through a near-deadly illness. But he has little appreciation. She is only a female. As to Kim, he does not want to be encumbered by the wounded boy, and he expects, even hopes, that the boy will die. When Kim survives the old peasant wants him as a worker and provider of luxuries.

The old curmudgeon is the most lifelike, the most human, of the three main characters in *I Am the Clay*. He is like a crotchety grandfather or a great uncle most of us have known: flawed, difficult, superstitious, and

opinionated, but someone whose determination to live evokes admiration and even affection.

Yet Potok has the old peasant undergo what the Classical Athenian
Aristotle called *anagnorisis*—self-recognition and a turn from hate to love.
Near the end of the novel he realizes that he cares a little for Kim and
that he will miss the boy even though there is no blood bond between
them.

THEMATIC ISSUES

The husband and wife are nameless. They are meant to symbolize the
basic unit of human community, a man and a woman. They seldom
speak to each other. Their life is constant work for mere subsistence.
They are not affectionate. But they need each other and are committed
to each other. At first Kim is a point of contention. The old man does
not want the burden of caring for the wounded child. The old woman
will not desert the gift and the challenge fate has given her. Eventually
the boy serves as a catalyst for the relationship. He gives the couple a
reason for surviving beyond saving themselves for a few more months
or years of life. Kim will become a poet or scholar who will help to
rebuild the ravished land. He has a destiny and the old people have
made that destiny possible.

For the first time in Potok's fiction, life appears to be a test. We cannot
know the purpose of our existence, but Potok in *I Am the Clay* themati-
cally implies that the purpose is there although it may never be revealed
to us. Compassion, cooperation, and belief in the continuity of life—even
the daily presence of the past—are the sinews necessary in order to endure what must be endured: existential suffering. The seeming random-
ness of life on an indifferent planet is not the end of meaning but the
beginning.

STYLISTIC AND LITERARY DEVICES

Potok adopts a very simple, spare linguistic style. The novel reads as
if it were a sensitive, rather literal translation of the speech and thought
of Asian people from an ancient agricultural society. A brilliant touch:
we even experience the mighty and terrible modern engines of war
through the baffled perceptions of the old peasant couple.

Potok's descriptive powers are at his best in *I Am the Clay* as he paints what Irving Abrahamson, in *Chicago Tribune Books*, calls "a dangerous world: troops in retreat; long processions of refugees, jeeps, trucks and tanks on the go; helicopters whirling overhead; jets streaking by" (6).

The significant iterative image in *I Am the Clay* is the Cross. Red crosses on ambulances, trucks, and medical tents, as well as some white crosses stud the novel. The old peasant woman makes the sign of the Cross several times, not knowing the meaning of the action. It is a good luck charm for her, and she has been lucky both in surviving as long as she had, and, more important, saving the life of her surrogate son Kim Sin Gyu who is part of the future of the Korean people. One senses that in her heart she feels fulfilled because ancestral spirits have given her back her son.

A DECONSTRUCTIONIST READING OF *I AM THE CLAY*

What Is Deconstruction?

Deconstruction is an analytical tool to show how literary works make and unmake themselves at the same time. It was devised in the late 1960s by Jacques Derrida, a French professor of philosophy who coined the term. He set out to prove that language is peculiarly circular or self-referential. That is, the language in a story does not really refer to a hard, fixed reality outside the pages but may have several possible meanings and may refer to the "reality" in other works. Furthermore, words are not the things they supposedly represent. The association of a word with a thing is arbitrary. It may depend on context or upon history.

Thus the meaning of a novel, for example, is indeterminate. The novel may have several meanings that may even undermine each other. Readings may change from age to age or person to person. A novel is not a solid; it is liquid. Its language is locked into a linguistic system while metaphors flow back and forth on the crests of "meanings."

For deconstructionists the readings of the literary work are everything. Author and historical background are secondary. Deconstruction liberates a literary work from authority by recognizing its indeterminacy. Undecidability is a virtue. One does not have to choose, only spoon out the choices onto the plate. Deconstruction enriches the feast of reading, and it is often irreverent fun.

The Reading

All dialogue in *I Am the Clay* is "Korean" except when Kim, having learned some English, is talking with the Jewish chaplain. That is, Potok creates a linguistic pattern that is supposed to have a Korean flavor. Although generally effective for an uncritical reading, the author's use of "Korean" takes on a certain pidgin English quality that upon reflection seems condescending to an ancient and sophisticated culture. The vocabulary is to a large extent monosyllabic. Ostensibly, this emphasizes the simplicity of the old couple, but after all, the languages of people in the developing world are no more or less limited than languages in the developed world. Potok means no slur, but is simply following in the prose traditions of colonialism that many writers like Edgar Rice Burroughs used to portray native peoples speaking without metaphors, similes, analogies, colloquialisms, and so forth.

For example: When the old peasant woman is questioned by a South Korean soldier about the boy she replies: "Yes, grandson. . . . His parents dead. Village burned" (103). Thus we are reminded that although writing is supposedly an imitation of speech it is really not, and especially not when the written speech is supposed to be a translation. We are reading a convention, possibly not a true translation. Aware of the problem, Potok limits dialogue to a minimum and relies on the descriptive third-person narration to create both character and atmosphere.

The fact that two of the three main characters in *I Am the Clay* are not named gives the characters a mythic or allegorical dimension that works against the specificity of the novel. Yet although the novel can be read as an allegory of human endurance, that reading is not privileged over any other. A more obvious reading, for example, is to see the novel as an ideological appeal for internationalism and multiculturalism. Potok does not want his readers to see people of other races, cultures, and religions as "others" in the sense of being alien, antagonists, or less than human.

I Am the Clay exerts pressure on society. Since most readers of the novels are relatively affluent Americans and Europeans, the overt anti-war political message and the call for recognition of the commonality of the human experience engenders certain feelings of guilt. Many American readers will feel and then reject guilt for the destruction brought to Korea in the United Nations' successful attempt to save South Korea nearly fifty years ago. This rejection then distances the reader from the intended empathy.

Other readers will think that the conflict between the merciless real world and the benign, timeless, spiritual world is resolved too patently with the flimsily motivated intercession of a clerical person, the Jewish chaplain. He serves as a plot closer and provider of an unlikely ending for the purpose of tidy packaging and putting the reader's conscience at ease.

A somewhat negative aspect of *I Am the Clay* in this post-colonial era is that Kim is rescued from illiteracy and poverty by a Western outsider, an army chaplain, a superior person from the sophisticated, developed world. This smacks of paternalism associated with missionaries and colonialism. Although they came as liberators, the Americans keep themselves separate, expect the Koreans to learn English while they seem not to attempt Korean, and generally behave as overlords. Readers in the developing world today read *I Am the Clay* quite differently than do most Americans or Europeans.

Bibliography

WORKS BY CHAIM POTOK

Fiction

Novels

References in the text are to the first edition listed.

The Book of Lights. New York: Knopf, 1981; New York: Fawcett, 1982.
The Chosen. New York: Simon and Schuster, 1967; Greenwich: Fawcett, 1967.
Davita's Harp. New York: Knopf, 1985; New York: Fawcett, 1986.
The Gift of Asher Lev. New York: Knopf, 1990; New York: Fawcett, 1991.
I Am the Clay. New York: Knopf, 1992; New York: Fawcett, 1997.
In the Beginning. New York: Knopf, 1975; Greenwich: Fawcett, 1975.
My Name Is Asher Lev. New York: Knopf, 1972; Greenwich: Fawcett, 1972.
The Promise. New York: Knopf, 1969; New York: Fawcett, 1969.

Short Fiction in Periodicals

"The Cats of 37 Alfasi Street." *American Judaism*, Fall 1996: 12–29; *World Over*, 27 October 1967: 12–13.
"The Dark Place Inside." *Dimensions*, Fall 1967: 35–39.
"The Fallen." *Hadassah Magazine* 55.4 (December 1973): 6–7.
"The Gifts of Andrea." *Seventeen*, October 1982: 152–53, 168, 171.
"Isabel." *The Kenyon Review* 20.3–4 (1998): 77.

"Max." *New England Review* 19.2 (1998): 33.
"Reflections on a Bronx Street." *Reconstructionist* 30.13 (30 October 1964): 13–20.
"A Tale of Two Soldiers." *Ladies Home Journal*, December 1981: 16, 18–19.
"The Trope Teacher Novella" *TriQuarterly* 101 (1998): 15.

Children's Literature

The Sky of Now. New York: Knopf, 1995.
The Tree of Here. New York: Knopf, 1993.
Zebra and Other Stories. New York: Knopf, 1998.

Nonfiction

Books

The Gates of November: Chronicles of the Slepak Family. New York: Knopf, 1996.
Isaac Stern: My First Seventy-Nine Years. New York: Knopf, 1991.
Theo Tobiasse: Artist in Exile. New York: Rizzoli International, 1986.
Wanderings: Chaim Potok's History of the Jews. New York: Knopf, 1978; New York: Fawcett, 1980.

Articles

"The Age of Permanent Apocalypse." *Pennsylvania Gazette*, June 1983: 55–58.
"The Bad News." *Philadelphia Magazine*, 79 (September 1988): 89.
"The Bible Inspired Art." *New York Times Magazine*, October 1982: 58–68.
"Culture Confrontation in Urban America: A Writer's Beginning." *Literature and the Urban Experience*, ed. Michael C. Jaye and Ann Chalmers Watts. New Brunswick, NJ: Rutgers University Press, 1981: 161–167.
"The First Eighteen Years." *Studies in American Jewish Literature* 4 (1985): 100–106.
"The Invisible Map of Meaning: A Writer's Confrontations." *TriQuarterly* 84 (Spring 1992): 17.
"Jews of the 1970s." *Ladies Home Journal*, December 1969: 134.
"Martin Buber and the Jews." *Commentary* 41 (March 1966): 43–49.
"Miracles for a Broken Planet." *McCall's*, December 1972: 36.
"The Mourners of Yehezkel Kaufmann." *Conservative Judaism* 18.2 (1964): 1–9.
"The Mourning Road." *Philadelphia Magazine* 89 (November 1998): 96.
"The Naturalism of Sidney Hook." *Conservative Judaism* 18.2 (1964): 40–52.
"The State of Jewish Belief." *The Conditions of Jewish Belief: A Symposium*. New York: Macmillan, 1966: 171–179.
"Teaching the Holocaust." *Philadelphia Magazine* 73 (April 1982): 130–145.

GENERAL INFORMATION AND CRITICISM

Abramson, Edward A. *Chaim Potok*. Boston: Twayne, 1986.

Allen, William M. *Chaim Potok Frequently Asked Questions* 1997. online: http://www.lasierra.edu/~ballen/potok/Potok.faqs.html.

Berger, Alan. *Crisis and Covenant: The Holocaust in American Jewish Fiction*. Albany: SUNY Press, 1985.

Del Fattore, Joan. "Women as Scholars in Chaim Potok's Novels." *Studies in American Jewish Literature* 4 (1984): 52–61.

Glicksberg, Charles F. "The Religious Revival in Contemporary Literature." *Western Humanities Review*, Winter 1957: 65–75.

Kauvar, Elaine M. "An Interview with Chaim Potok." *Contemporary Literature* 27.3 (Fall 1986): 291–317.

Kremer, S. Lillian. "Eternal Light: The Holocaust and the Revival of Judaism and Jewish Civilization in the Fiction of Chaim Potok." *Witness Through Imagination: Jewish American Holocaust Literature*. Detroit: Wayne State University Press, 1989: 300–323.

———. "Chaim Potok." In *American Novelists Since World War II: Dictionary of Literary Biography*, ed. James R. Giles and Wanda H. Giles. Detroit: Gale, 1985. Vol. 152, 202–215.

Leviant, Curt. "The Hasid as American Hero." *Midstream*, 13 November 1967: 76–80.

Marovitz, Sanford. "Freedom, Faith, and Fanaticism: Cultural Conflict in the Novels of Chaim Potok." *Studies in American Jewish Literature* 4 (1986): 129–140.

Purcell, William F. "Potok's Fathers and Sons." *Studies in American Literature* 26 (1989): 75–92.

Walden, Daniel. "Chaim Potok: A *Zwischenmensch* Adrift in the Cultures." *Studies in American Jewish Literature* 4 (1984): 19–25.

Woodman, Katherine Ann. "Secular and Sacred in the Art of Chaim Potok." Ph.D. diss. University of Alberta, 1993.

Zlotnick, Joan. "The Chosen Borough: Chaim Potok's Brooklyn." *Studies in American Jewish Literature* 4 (1984): 13–18.

BIOGRAPHICAL INFORMATION

Pfeiffer, Pat. "The World of Chaim Potok." *Inside*, Winter 1981: 54–55, 102–104.

Stern, David. "Two Worlds." *Commentary*, October 1972: 102, 104.

Walden, Daniel. "Chaim Potok." *Twentieth-Century American Jewish Fiction Writers* 28 (1984): 232–243.

REVIEWS AND CRITICISM

The Chosen

Grebstein, Sheldon. "The Phenomenon of the Really Jewish Best Seller: Potok's *The Chosen.*" *Studies in American Jewish Literature* 1 (Spring 1975): 23–31.

Harap, Louis. *In the Mainstream: The Jewish Presence in Twentieth-Century American Literature, 1950s–1980s* Westport, CT: Greenwood, 1987: 162–164.

Toynbee, Phillip. Review of *The Chosen. New Republic* 156 (June 1967): 21.

The Promise

Bandler, Michael S. "A Sequel to *The Chosen.*" *Christian Science Monitor*, 16 December 1969: 13.

Freedman, Richard. Review of *The Promise. Washington Post Book World*, 14 September 1969: 3.

Nissenson, Hugh. "The Jews Have Long Since Embarked: *The Promise.*" *New York Times Book Review*, 14 September 1969: 5, 21.

My Name Is Asher Lev

Ahrens, Henry. "Tale From an Archetypal Ocean: Potok's *My Name Is Asher Lev.*" *Studies in American Jewish Literature* 12 (1993): 42–49.

Davenport, Guy. "Collision with the Outside World." *New York Times Book Review*, 16 April 1972: 5, 18.

Dembo, L. S. *The Monological Jew: A Literary Study.* Madison, WI: University of Wisconsin Press, 1988: 112–116.

Forbes, Cheryl. "Judaism Under the Secular Umbrella." *Christianity Today*, 22 September 1978: 14–21.

Kauvar, Elaine M. "An Interview With Chaim Potok." *Contemporary Literature* 27.3 (1986): 291–317.

Milch, Robert J. Review of *My Name Is Asher Lev. Saturday Review*, 15 April 1972: 65–66.

Pinsker, Sanford. "The Crucifixion of Chaim Potok/The Excommunication of Asher Lev: Art and the Hasidic World." *Studies in American Jewish Literature* 4 (1985): 39–51.

True, Warren. "Potok and Joyce: The Artist and His Culture." *Studies in American Jewish Literature* 2 (1982): 181–190.

Uffen, Ellen. "*My Name Is Asher Lev*: Chaim Potok's Portrait of the Young Hasid as Artist." *Studies in American Jewish Literature* 2 (1982): 174–180.

In the Beginning

Dame, Enid. "Bellow and Potok: The Saving Force." *Congress Monthly*, April 1976: 20–22.

Keimig, H. S. *"In the Beginning." Best Seller* 38 (January 1976): 302.

Merkin, Daphne. "Why Is Potok Popular?" *Commentary*, February 1976: 73–75.

The Book of Lights

Manuel, D. C. "Potok's Journey Toward Light." *Christian Science Monitor*, 14 October 1981, B4.

Rosenbaum, S. N. "Review of *The Book of Lights." Christian Century* 99 (17 February 1982): 184.

Soll, Will. "Chaim Potok's *Book of Lights*: Reappropriating Kabbalah in the Nuclear Age." *Religion and Literature* 21 (1989): 111–135.

Davita's Harp

Cowan, Paul. "The Faith of Her Childhood." *New York Times Book Review*, 31 March 1985: 12–13.

Dos Passos, John. *1919*. New York: Grosset and Dunlap, 1932.

Hoffman, Marcia R. *"Davita's Harp." Library Journal* 15 (February 1985): 180.

The Gift of Asher Lev

Fitch, Katherine. Review of *The Gift of Asher Lev. School Library Journal* 36 (September 1990): 268.

Morton, Brian. "The Gift of Asher Lev." (London) *Times Literary Supplement*, 2 November 1990: 1182.

Stiller, Nikki. "Art Is an Affliction." *New York Times Book Review*, 13 May 1990: 29.

I Am the Clay

Cheyette, Brian. "The Second East." (London) *Times Literary Supplement*, 27 November 1992: 21.

Gropman, Jackie. Review of *I Am the Clay. School Library Journal* 38 (December 1992): 148.

Abrahamson, Irving. Review of *"I Am The Clay." Chicago Tribune Books*, 17 May 1992: 6, 501.

Zingman, Barbara Gold. *"I Am the Clay." New York Times Book Review*, 28 June 1992: 18.

PLAYS

The Chosen. Musical adaptation of the book. Premiered off-Broadway in New
    York, 6 January 1988. A dramatic version was produced in Philadelphia
    and Pittsburgh, Spring 1999. *Out of the Depths*. Drama in two parts. Pre-
    miered in Philadelphia, 17 April–13 May 1990.
The Play of Lights. One-act play. Premiered in Philadelphia, 13 May 1992.
Sins of the Father: The Carnival and *The Gallery*. Two one-act plays. Premiered in
    Philadelphia, 24 May 1990. (*The Carnival* comes from the carnival story
    early in *The Promise. The Gallery* comes from the gallery scene in *My Name
    Is Asher Lev*.)

FILM ADAPTATION

The Chosen. Dir. Jeremy Paul Kagan. 1982.

Index

About the Author

SANFORD STERNLICHT teaches in Syracuse University's English Department and Judaic Studies Program. He is a series editor for Syracuse University Press. His recent books on modern writers include *Stephen Spender, Jean Rhys,* and *All Things Herriot: James Herriot and His Peaceable Kingdom.* He also frequently writes on poetry and Irish literature. His essay on Padraic Colum appeared in *Modern Irish Writers: A Bio-Critical Sourcebook* (Greenwood 1997). He has contributed articles to many periodicals including *College English, Harvard Magazine, Writer's Digest, Calcutta Review,* and *Renaissance Quarterly.*

Critical Companions to Popular Contemporary Writers
Second Series

Rudolfo A. Anaya *by Margarite Fernandez Olmos*

Maya Angelou *by Mary Jane Lupton*

Louise Erdrich *by Lorena L. Stookey*

Ernest J. Gaines *by Karen Carmean*

John Irving *by Josie P. Campbell*

Garrison Keillor *by Marcia Songer*

Jamaica Kincaid *by Lizabeth Paravisini-Gebert*

Barbara Kingsolver *by Mary Jean DeMarr*

Terry McMillan *by Paulette Richards*

Larry McMurtry *by John M. Reilly*

Toni Morrison *by Missy Dehn Kubitschek*

Amy Tan *by E. D. Huntley*

Anne Tyler *by Paul Bail*

Leon Uris *by Kathleen Shine Cain*

Critical Companions to Popular Contemporary Writers
First Series—*also available on CD-ROM*

V. C. Andrews
  by E. D. Huntley

Tom Clancy
  by Helen S. Garson

Mary Higgins Clark
  by Linda C. Pelzer

Arthur C. Clarke
  by Robin Anne Reid

James Clavell
  by Gina Macdonald

Pat Conroy
  by Landon C. Burns

Robin Cook
  by Lorena Laura Stookey

Michael Crichton
  by Elizabeth A. Trembley

Howard Fast
  by Andrew Macdonald

Ken Follett
  by Richard C. Turner

John Grisham
  by Mary Beth Pringle

James Herriot
  by Michael J. Rossi

Tony Hillerman
  by John M. Reilly

John Jakes
  by Mary Ellen Jones

Stephen King
  by Sharon A. Russell

Dean Koontz
  by Joan G. Kotker

Robert Ludlum
  by Gina Macdonald

Anne McCaffrey
  by Robin Roberts

Colleen McCullough
  by Mary Jean DeMarr

James A. Michener
  by Marilyn S. Severson

Anne Rice
  by Jennifer Smith

Tom Robbins
  *by Catherine E. Hoyser and
  Lorena Laura Stookey*

John Saul
  by Paul Bail

Erich Segal
  by Linda C. Pelzer

Gore Vidal
  by Susan Baker and Curtis S. Gibson